Rise Up to Greatness

A Young Women's Devotional

Created by
Selina Sosa

Selina Sosa
Dallas, Texas

Copyright © 2017 Selina Sosa. All rights reserved. No portion of this book may be reproduced mechanically, electronically, or by any other means, including photocopying, without written permission of the publisher. It is illegal to copy this book, post it to a website, or distribute it by any other means without permission.

Limits of Liability
The author and publisher shall not be liable for your misuse of this material. This book is strictly for informational and educational purposes.

Disclaimer
The purpose of this book is to educate and entertain. The author and/or publisher do not guarantee that anyone following these techniques, suggestions, tips, ideas, or strategies will become successful. The author and/or publisher shall have neither liability nor responsibility to anyone with respect to any loss of damage caused, or alleged to be caused, directly or indirectly by the information contained in this book.

Editing and Layout: The Self-Publishing Maven
Formatting: Deepak Gupta
Book Cover: Okomota, The Design Lab

Printed in the United States of America

Acknowledgements

My sincere gratitude to the women of this project who said yes in partnering with me and the vision. Ladies, you took on a challenge said yes so that others might be blessed.

To my husband Fernando Sosa, for always believing and supporting anything I want to do. You never say no, because you are aware of my passion and fire for what I love and you never want to burn that fire out. Not to mention you know I would do it anyway! I love you.

To my amazing, handsome sons, thank you for always believing in me and sharing a bit of me with everyone of else. I know it was hard, but you let me be a mom to others when you just wanted me to be a mom to you. I love you more than words will ever express. You are my "sunshine", my "yaya" and my "chunka pie". I hope I have made you proud. A mis abuelos y mamá, si no fuera por ustedes, no podría ser la esposa o la madre que soy hoy. Gracias por cuidarme y siempre creer en mí. Los amo a todos.

Thank you, Shelly Cassady for trusting God, me and diving into my craziness even when you knew I was ready to walk away.

Thank you, Dr. Té Colston, for immediately dropping a word and sticking with me every step of the way.

Thank you, Robin Devonish for reminding me that if I see a need, it is okay to meet it even if there is opposition.

Dedication

I dedicate this book to every young woman that was made to feel like she did not matter or was not important due to the color of her skin, socio-economic background, and cultural upbringing. You matter; you can and will succeed no matter the obstacle before you.

Prologue

My Year of Tears

Growing up I never thought about my future beyond what I wanted for myself. For me, it was to have a career, be married and to have kids. I never thought about all the things that can go wrong, who would? My grandmother the wise woman that she is would always tell me things like, never say never, or don't say that won't happen to you because you just do not know what the future holds. I now know she was right, but back then I would never believe those words for my life.

You see the past five years have been the most difficult I've ever dealt with. Issues at home with my kids, a rocky marriage, a year's worth of a health scares in my personal life, almost losing my grandmother, and in the most recent year almost losing my mom. Most people had no idea that I was dealing with any of this. Not because I was afraid to share, but frankly I don't trust many people. Most people just want to know your business to tell it when it's your story to tell.

In 2016 I couldn't hold anything back. The strong woman I was raised to be had taken her last whip to the back. While I would laugh, smile, and go out with my friends, truthfully on inside I was falling apart so badly that I forgot to go to the one place where I knew my strength would be restored. I stopped praying as I should. You see through all those other years, I knew where to run so whenever something was falling apart, I prayed, I fasted I rallied around people who I knew would genuinely go to war with me. That all changed in 2016, I lost focus, and I spent a good part of the year in tears. I had to come to terms with a possibility of loss; a life totally changed I couldn't eat or sleep. My life was a mess, and the one source of strength I had I could not connect with. I found myself in such a selfish place and was running nowhere fast. Even in all that mess and uncertainty of what could or would happen I still managed to cry out to my Father and just say, please don't leave me. I know your hand is upon me, but just don't leave me. At this point even asking for prayer was a challenge and trying to explain to others what I was going through was proving to be difficult. Just get over it, move on, and snap out of it, let go. I loathed those words. When you are facing something so deep that you cannot even see the light from the ditch you are climbing out of, the worst thing you can hear are those words. I appreciated and understood why people said it. However, you do not know how deep roots go just to tell someone to let go. You see, what occurs in our personal life doesn't matter to someone who needs something from you. You have to get up every day and do your duties because people depend on you. In the end, however, the only ones that do matter are the ones that stay with you and pray with you; your family and close knit friends. Those who no matter how many times you rattled off the issue to them and they were probably tired of hearing it, they still listened and stood with you. They understood the value of your heart and the moment you were going through. I know my tears for this year were not in vain, you see the bible tells me the following in Psalms 56:8, "You keep track of all my sorrows. You have collected all my tears in your bottle. You have recorded each one in your book."

My tears were not in vain but were necessary. Although I prayed and always went to the throne of God, there were a few issues that I would keep to myself. Issues I felt I would be better at handling than God so I would keep those to myself. So in 2016 at the height of all that God was doing, I had a spiritual breakdown. All the junk, hurt, anger that I repressed, came out like a tsunami devouring everything and almost everyone in my path. I could not do it anymore. I had to let it ALL GO.
I will never forget when I spoke to my pastor's wife and said to her, "I am just tired of crying," and I will never forget what she said. "Crying is good; it is the language of the soul when you don't know what to say your tears speak for you." Well, apparently I had a lot I could not say because in all honestly in 2016 there was not a morning, afternoon, or night I wasn't in tears. How is that even possible, no idea? Even on the day that I wrote this, I cried.

I am still healing, and it is still hard, but my Father says He has collected all my tears in a bottle and has recorded each one in His book. So for every person who did not care about my tears, or for the times I thought my tears were in vain, my heavenly Father made sure to remind me that He knows my pain and the reason for each drop that fell from my eyes. He also knows the very cause and the person who was behind it. Wow! In that I find comfort. It gives me peace; it restores my desire to pray. Nothing that I have gone through has escaped the glance of my Father, and nothing you have gone through has escaped Him either.

Father, I pray for my sister reading this today, and I ask that you fill and cover her with your garment of love. Sing over her on the nights that are filled with tears. I pray that the Holy Spirit would comfort and embrace her with an overwhelming love never felt before. I pray against any form of pride that would keep her from releasing those very things that could entrap her in bitterness, or anger or depression. I pray a special agape love and that it would radiate on her face as each new day passes. Lord remind her today that you hold every tear and you are aware of the reasons for each drop; even if her tears were a floodgate that ran together, you would see every drop and count it. Oh, Lord, I ask for your hand to hold your daughter. Give her assurance that you have not only loved her but also forgiven her and that if her tears are drawn out of guilt, you will still take them and put them in a bottle. Father give her wisdom, peace and restore her life to what you intended in Jesus name, Amen.

Contents

Love 10
    Unconditional love 11
    Just In Time 15
    Jesus is Enough 18
    Laughter 21
    Fearful 23
    The Sixth Love Language 27

Pain 30
    Losing Someone Special 31
    It's Going To Be Okay 33
    Get Up...Enough is Enough! 36
    Salty 42
    Suffering 45
    It Is Possible 50
    Conquering Loneliness 53

Spirit 55
    He Wants Your Worship! 56
    Fight or Die! 60
    Rotten Fruit 67
    His Joy 70
    Christ is The Invisible Image 73
    Letting Go 76
    Beware Of The Weeds 80

Family 86
    Reclaimed My Marriage 87
    One Nation Under God 90
    The Fight for Community 96
    Secret Petition 99
    Trusting Others = Trusting God 101
    Please Don't Forget Me 103

Rise Up to Greatness

Freedom 106
    Accepting Every Season in Life 107
    Bound to be Set Free 110
    The King Who Saved Me 115
    Steps to Freedom 119
    Trim Your Hedges 122
    Mind Renewing Faith Lavished With Love 125

Epilogue 129
Co-Author Devotions 130
About the Authors 133

Love

"A loving heart is the truest wisdom"
–Charles Dickens

Unconditional love

Girl meets boy, falls in love. Girl breaks boy's heart. They break up. Boy comes back breaks girl's heart. Girl meets another boy gets pregnant, but the first boy comes back and makes a promise. A very important promise, a covenant if you will, only to never follow through on that promise; disappears without a word or trace.

Let me explain something about love! It is fickle! It stinks! It is painful! It can be hard to understand! However, equally, it is wonderful when expressed unconditionally. When young, it's hard to understand love because we're too selfish! We want all we can get without really thinking about the ramifications and the pain we can cause due to selfish behavior. That young person was me! I can't express here how I hurt this person, that is for another time. What I do know is that my selfish heart got in the way of what I believed was truly a loving relationship.

When my ex-boyfriend disappeared without a trace, I was devastated. I couldn't for the life of me understand why anyone would make a promise to be with you, to marry you, only to just walk away. Here I was, a teen mother already confused trying to raise a son and found my heart in pieces. How I survived that time without the Lord I will never understand but oh did He have a master plan. You see God loved me, but I didn't know it yet. I spent the next three months of my life an angry girl, BITTER. I tell you when you're hurting, men come out of the woodwork. It felt like I was the only girl left on earth because every type of guy was approaching me, but I definitely wasn't interested. I would look at them, size them up and then count out their weaknesses like dollar bills. I was broken so I would try and find what was broken in every guy I met. To me, they were never worth my time, and in my mind, would hurt me just like the last one did. I would never be the same or so I thought!

One night a bunch of girlfriends and I went out dancing and that is where I met him! The man that I wasn't looking to be with; who would change my life, came in like a knight to rescue me. He was a man who was broken, but I was not willing to break him down like I did the rest.

When we met, we were both in pretty bad places; he was done with a relationship that left him heartbroken. Two broken people, see the pattern yet? I expressed to him I didn't want anything serious at that moment, and I certainly didn't want him to meet my son. I wasn't sure how things would work out between us and that decision was best for all of us. He agreed! He also stated he didn't want anything serious. I laugh now as I think back on that moment. It was all a set up by God!

We met July of 1994, and by that November we were engaged and married in June of 1995. Happy ending right? Wrong, Selina was still broken, and because she did not give herself a chance to heal from that one relationship, she brought all her insecurities into her marriage, and it looked like this:

Me: "Do you love me?"
Him: "Of course, I married you."
Me: "That doesn't mean anything; people marry for the wrong reasons all the time."
Him: "Well not me!"
Me: "Are you going to leave me?"
Him: (annoyed) "Do you want me to leave you?"
Me: Stays silent because now I am pushing him, it must be me. There is something wrong with me.

These types of conversations would go on for years. I began to look at myself and believed I wasn't pretty enough, good enough, smart enough just never enough. At the time I couldn't connect the real reason why I was feeling the way I was. My behavior stemmed from a deep hurt concerning my ex and the rejections in my life.

Don't get me wrong I was raised with much love and affection. My grandparents raised me and while mom was always a part of my life, my dad wasn't. I could never wrap my head around why he wasn't a part of my life when he had other kids and was active in their lives. What was wrong with me that he couldn't be around me? This would translate into every area of my life when someone didn't want to be a part of it. Rejection was a terrible feeling, and no matter how much love I was shown by my family, there was a void. So when my husband was having a bad week, a bad day or just needed a moment to himself, I translated that into rejection; he doesn't love me and would rather be with someone else.

It was not until I gave my heart to the Lord that I started to understand love. Real love! Love that says you hurt me, but I forgive you and I won't hold anything against you. Love that says, live your dream out first and I will support you even if I can't live out mine. Love that says, you may not like what I am about to tell you, but because I love you I'm not going to walk away, but I am going to tell you all the reasons why this is not going to work. True love says I will lay down my life for you even if, it will never matter to you.

Wow! You see during this whole time I never explained what my husband did do to express his love. He let me be free! I could always be myself around him, and since you don't know me I have to let you in on a secret, I am crazy. I LOVE to have fun. I love to entertain people, have them over, have grown up sleepovers, dance, and just be silly. He never once criticized me, he may have called me crazy, but understood that I was being me. What he received was the best part of me, the authentic me, which was the best for his life. Nothing less! Every crazy idea I've had has never been met with a no. He has said that I am crazy, but never said no.

You see God did the same thing by allowing me to go through my moments of pain, hurt, and despair waiting for me to come to Him. He tried to restore me, but I kept running. Even when I had Him, I kept that one thing that hurt inside of me and from Him until it all came crashing in. I was forced to stand before His altar and give every piece of my heart to Him. Man did that hurt; I relived every terrible moment for months. God knew that whoever was in my life needed to let me be me so that He could do His greatest work in me. My deepest hurt would show to almost destroying me again, but instead, God stepped in and showed me forgiveness and love in a way I had not experienced before. Love with no strings attached, a rare unbiased love. Love that said Selina, if you just give me the one thing that hurt, I promise you will never be the same. Choose me, Selina, leave everything behind, choose me, and trust me. My heart is warm as I write these parts because no one ever understood my pain, but God did. He knew it so well. All He ever wanted to do was show me His love, but I was too busy trying to restore a love that I thought was genuine the wrong way. How foolish of me. Romans 8:38-39(NLT) reads this:

"And I am convinced that nothing can ever separate us from God's love. Neither death nor life, neither angels nor demons, neither our fears for today nor our worries about tomorrow—not even the powers of hell can separate us from God's love. No power in the sky above or in the earth below—indeed, nothing in all creation will ever be able to separate us from the love of God that is revealed in Christ Jesus our Lord."

Nothing can separate me from His love, NOTHING. No past sin, no fear, even if I break His heart, He still loves me. So I live my life daily trying to not break the heart of God. His love according to scripture is unconditional for me, so why would I want to do anything to break His heart when He would never break mine? God keeps His promise. His word is His promise and the idea that He will never leave me, always love every moment is the unconditional love I desired but was too broken to receive it until I let it all go.

Let's Pray
Father, I thank you for your unconditional love toward my life. I pray that the young woman reading this that may feel unloved, not worthy or that has been rejected would begin to feel your unbiased, compassionate, restorative love. I pray that when the enemy speaks through the voices of others, she would recognize it immediately and put a stop to negative thoughts. God, let her be reminded that nothing could ever separate her from your love. I speak life into the spirit of every woman and young lady reading this now, and I ask that they would feel your joy, your happiness and most importantly your love in Jesus name. Amen!

Just In Time

"Death, where is your victory? Death, where is your sting?"
1 Corinthians 15:55

Is she going to die? Will I be left to face this ongoing resentment I have towards my mother in which I have secretly held within for all these years? These were haunting thoughts I struggled with for a period of about 15 months. I knew they were not Christ-centered thoughts but I couldn't negate my feelings. They were surfacing more now than ever. How could I have compassion for someone who didn't love me? Someone who said she was waiting for me to die because I was on borrowed time. According to the spiritualist she often visited, I was supposed to die at the age of sixteen years old. I often visited my mother who was clinically diagnosed with Adrenal Cancer. Her diagnosis wasn't a surprise to me for The Lord had revealed it to me in a dream with great detail.

He revealed to me that my mother had a black shapeless mass in her stomach. He stated in the dream if she didn't repent, she would surely die. My mother once served the Lord but had turned away to serve idols. I remember waking up with tears in my eyes and reaching for the phone to call my mother. I frantically tried to explain to her what the Lord had said in the dream, but my mother mocked me and hung up the phone.

A month later she went to the doctor's office because she was feeling exhausted. My mother underwent several studies at Sloan-Kettering Hospital to which the doctor gave her a final report; she was diagnosed with Adrenal Cancer. There was no cure or treatment for it at that time.

When I found out she was visiting the doctor's office I asked her what was wrong. She refused to tell me her condition and denied the doctor's report. I really didn't know if the denial was because of cancer or because of what the Lord had revealed to me. Either way,

I knew this was her coping mechanism to handle her misfortune.

My mother was placed in Hospice Care, where she reconciled with the Lord Jesus Christ. The Lord had ministered to me and said "this is a season to intercede for your mother. I will recall her past sins so she may be able to ask forgiveness for all those she has wronged."

I witnessed emotional healing as she apologized to family members. The Holy Spirit was operating under the power of restoration, so much so that she apologized to my husband for trying to sabotage our marriage; always saying he could leave me if he wasn't happy, that they'd remain friends. Although I was pleased to see my mother say sorry to others, unfortunately, her asking for forgiveness never found its way to me. Even after this amazing renewal, I still didn't matter in her eyes.

Through prayer and intercession, I made peace in my heart that I didn't need to hear "I'm sorry Haydee". It was an exhausting journey. During my mother's last days, she was constantly harassed by her husband, who was strongly into Santeria and often tried to force her to pray to idols. I purposely would flood her room with worship music and read the word of God to her, while my stepfather stood at her doorway, almost as if he couldn't enter. I reminded my mother that during her illness, she was still battling forces that wanted to drag her back to relying on dead idols. I warned her to be watchful, meditate, and pray; not to allow him to chant over her.

One morning before visiting my mother, I decided to go workout and release my stress. While I was jogging on the treadmill, I observed the people walking by and felt an overflow of God's presence to the point that I had to stop and be still. The Lord revealed to me that my mother could not love me, as she didn't love herself; nor was she loved by her own mother. My mother was a product of rape. I heard the voice of the Lord say to me "Haydee, the enemy stole you and your mother's relationship. He targeted you from adolescence. Remember, the devil came to steal, kill, and destroy". (John 10:10 DBY) I was flooded with God's overwhelming presence and began to weep, feeling a release from my spirit. No longer did I feel the burden, I was eager to visit my mother. I gathered my belongings and proceeded to visit her at the hospital, not realizing that this would be our last moments together.

She smiled at me as I entered her room, to which I smiled back. I no longer looked at her with pity, I was proud of her, knowing her salvation was guaranteed. Lying in her sickbed, she was at peace. The doctor escorted me out to the hallway asking me if I wanted to waive any further medical treatment, to which I answered yes. My husband secretly prayed for her at her side and said "Jenny do not be afraid, be of good cheer. He's coming for you." A tear ran down her face, to which her eyes showed her understanding. I re-entered the room and recall feeling a still peace among us. I kissed my mother goodbye.

The next day while I was still in bed, I felt joy and sorrow in my spirit. The phone rang, with my grandmother on the line. "Your mother went in peace Haydee", to which I replied, "I know... I felt it." It was a Sunday morning, and I left on my way to church. I remember that service being one of the best services I've experienced. I couldn't help but smile and rejoice. I remember experiencing a light on my face as I prayed in church, having a vision of my mother in a youthful state. That experience left me overwhelmed and I was healed.

Let's Pray
Father God I pray for all those broken relationships between a mother and a daughter. I pray that there will be healing and what the enemy has tried to destroy, the Lord will mend. It is never too late to reconcile. All things are possible through Christ. Amen

Jesus is Enough

My entire life I've struggled with over thinking, over worrying, and under sleeping. I have spent many nights in my life, wide-awake, worrying about things that I couldn't control at three o'clock in the morning. I'm not talking about just my adult life; I did it as a child. I would stay up all night worrying about grades, friends, and family. I would keep myself up over irrational things and think that people were going to break into my house and kidnap me. I wish I could tell you that I learned how to work through those thoughts, but now that I'm an adult, the things I worry about are a lot more realistic and frequent.
The things I struggle with have a tendency of making me feel like my life is so hard. I believe we all have something in our lives that make us feel that way, but in certain moments I feel as if I'm the only one. I'm sure that if I talked to a professional about my issues, they would tell me that I have struggled with these things because of the way my life has played out thus far, especially as a child.

At an early age, my parents divorced. My father was given full custody of me and my mom completely disappeared out of my life for a few years. My dad had to learn how to be the one that financially supported our family, but also, how to be the nurturer. He had to learn how to do things like curling my hair and making sure I ate a warm meal. I had to learn how to do things like make acceptable meals, laundry, and clean up at an early age. My dad later remarried in life, but that also resulted in divorce. After that divorce, I was once again left figuring out how to do things to take care of myself. I'm sure someone would say that my instability in life caused all of the anxiety I deal with. I don't tell you these things to think I had a bad childhood, or that my parents weren't good parents. Also, I'm not sharing this to make anyone feel bad for me. I was very fortunate, and regardless, I think my parents are wonderful.

My mom later came back into my life, and we have mended our relationship. I admire my dad for always persevering and learning how to deal with the cards he was given. He is the hardest worker I know, and the best friend a girl could ask for. My father taught me so much about hard work, forgiveness, appreciation, and perseverance.

My childhood taught me a lot of lessons about life, sometimes at too young of an age. I was fully taking care of myself before I was even a teenager, which made it easy when I became an adult. The biggest lesson I had to learn was I needed God in my situation. I adore my parents, but I had to learn that the world and the sin in the world made them imperfect. I feel as if everyone has to learn that their parents are not perfect at some point in their life. But that was hard for me to accept. Once I learned to accept that my parents weren't perfect, but God was, all of the things I struggled with in life became a little easier. There is a reason that we call him our Heavenly Father. He is our ultimate parent.

Fast forward to today, I still struggle with stress, anxiety, and not sleeping. Unlike when I was a child, today I realize that God is enough for me in those moments. I have learned not to worry because God has taken care of it all and knows exactly how everything is going to work out. He's not surprised by anything that happens in our lives. Sometimes accepting this is easier said than done, but when I really rely on and trust Him, things become so much easier. I've learned how to pray in moments of anxiousness. I have had to learn that sometimes God is trying to teach me something in those moments where I am wide awake at three o'clock in the morning.

Again, we all have things in life that seem hard, make us feel like no one understands or can't relate to us. However, once we learn that God makes us whole in those moments, life becomes easier. Sweet sister, if you have struggled in this area, I pray that you learn to accept that He (Jesus) is enough. I promise your life will be much better once you do. God will fill every void and is your best friend, parent, teacher, and counselor. He will be there when you need Him. I encourage you to rely on God in every moment.

"Do not be anxious about anything, but in every situation, by prayer and petition, with thanksgiving, present your requests to God. And the peace of God, which transcends all understanding, will guard your hearts and your minds in Christ Jesus." Philippians 4:6-7 (NIV)

Below is an idea for a prayer to use. Please feel free to use these words, or use them as a guide of what to say during your reflection time with God.

<u>Let's Pray</u>
God, I ask that in this moment you would help me remember that You are enough, You complete me in every way, and can fill every void I will ever have. I know that sometimes I spend too much time worrying about things that you have already taken care of. I ask that you would forgive me for not always and fully trusting You. You've never failed me, and you always take care of me regardless of any situation. Thank you for being the perfect parent, friend, and counselor in my life. Thank for every blessing you give me, even though sometimes I am not even aware of the blessing that is coming. In Jesus name, Amen.

Laughter

"A merry heart does good, like medicine. But a broken spirit dries to the bone bones." Proverbs 17:2 (GNT)

One of my fondest childhood memories is my mother reading us a bedtime story. Every night at 8:00 p.m., she gathered all four of us around her bed. It tickled us pink to hear our mother read in English with her heavy Spanish accent. Her broken English healed her children in many ways and this was our special family time together, our "family tradition". For those few moments, it seemed that everything in our home was well. Sadly, the bedtime time story came to a sudden halt when she died. No one else gathered us to read us a story before bedtime after her passing. We could have never imagined the deep longing to hear her voice again.

It was seven months after my mother's death that I came down with a severe case of the mumps. The doctors prescribed medication and quarantine. Those were long and lonely hours. Those hours heightened the reality of my mother's absence; to say the least, quarantine deepened my sorrow.

My youngest brother Raul was introduced to the book, "The Little World of Don Carmillo." He found it very hysterical and it truly was. After he finished his homework, he would knock on my bedroom door wanting to read me one of the stories from the book. Raul was not concerned about getting sick but rather he wanted his sister to get well. Each night he came to "visit" me. The book was hilarious. Raul was not only my brother but also a friend in a very lonely time. He remembered his sister and didn't forget our family bedtime story tradition. Mom would have been proud of her son. The Lord visited me through my brother. The laughter did not make the mumps to disappear but it soothed not one but two aching hearts. My brother was the best medicine.

What I learned from that experience is, the Lord will send you a friend in your darkest moment, an understanding friend that identifies with your sorrow. Your friend knows when you should cry together but also when you need a good laugh. The gift of laughter will comfort your grieving heart.

Let's Pray
Father God, I am asking on behalf of my brothers and sisters that need the medicine of laughter. Send a friend that will lift up their spirit and cause them to forget their sorrow. Laughter is like a good medicine that helps us to feel better. You promised us that the joy of the Lord would be our strength. You are near to the brokenhearted. Bring the medicine of joy and laughter today and heal our aching hearts. We thank you for caring friends. We thank you for the gift of laughter in Jesus' name, Amen.

Fearful

"For God has not given us a spirit of fear, but of power and love and self-control." 2 Timothy 1:7 (ESV)

Fear is an emotion where we can relate. Fear can come to us in many different forms and have lasting effects if not dealt with. Some fears we may see as childish or silly, such as being afraid of the dark, being afraid of spiders, or even afraid of heights. While other fears may cast a larger shadow and hit deeper within the soul, such as fear of being alone, fear of what others might say or think about you, fear of failing or maybe even fear of exposing the skeletons in your closet. No matter the fear, we all can relate in some form or fashion. Allow me to share a few of my fearful failures.

Before I was married one of my biggest fears was being alone. I didn't trust the Lords' timing or His Word and worried that I would end up an old maid. Instead of being content with the Lord, I started to believe there was something wrong with me and that I wasn't good enough for anyone. The lies from the enemy penetrated my thoughts and I allowed fear to control me. Once I was in a relationship, I was afraid of being cheated on, afraid that he would lose interest and afraid of being dumped. I would try to hide my fear and insecurities, but it always got the best of me. It wasn't until I started reading and studying God's word that I began to understand my worth. I soon realized that my worth and identity was in the Lord. It didn't matter what some guy said or thought, what the Lord said about me was important!
Don't listen to the lies of the enemy for God personally "knit you together in your mother's womb" and you "are fearfully and wonderfully made" Psalms 139:13-14 ESV. After His word sunk into my heart, I began to notice my fear started to fade and my thought process improved. Staying plugged in His Word is crucial as a believer.

Now into the married life, my husband Joshua and I have

had our share of fear. Joshua was a police officer when we met and I knew then that I might be faced with the fear that accompanies all police wives and their family members. It was hard, but I tried not to worry; especially when I didn't hear from him or when I knew he had to work late into the night. It was a relief every time I heard the door shut in the early morning hours and the deadbolt lock. I was able to rest. Thankfully, the Lord protected him throughout his shifts. However, from his perspective, he was more fearful of failing, not being the best officer he could be, and of not being able to make a change in the community where he served. As he continued in his career, he longed to pursue other directions within law enforcement. Despite trying many different police departments, they all turned him down. Trying many different directions, he was having no luck and experiencing much rejection. The fear of failure began to creep in once again. Questioning the Lord, he repeatedly asked why and desperately sought to know which career path he was to pursue. Joshua had such a longing in his heart and firmly believed the career he had was what he was supposed to do. Little did we know that the Lord was tugging his heart in a completely different direction.

        In the summer of 2015, change started to happen. The Lord revealed the longing in Joshua's heart was being replaced with a calling to ministry.

We soon had confirmation after confirmation from different sources and we were completely blown away by the Lords' answers. Yet in raw honesty, even in the Lords' moving, we were fearful of Joshua leaving his job and being dependent on one income, fearful of not knowing enough and failing at what He was calling us to do. Despite our fear and faithlessness, the Lord has been faithful. We took a leap of faith and Joshua quit his job, started Bible school and has pursued ministry. The Lord has preserved and provided for us every step of the way. We have grown in the Lord and are excited to walk in His calling. If we would've allowed fear to control us and not have listened to the Lord's tugging, I believe we would be miserable. The enemy will try to use fear to distract you from the call of the Lord. However, fear can't control you once you make the decision to let go and let God.

Rise Up to Greatness

    As of recent, Joshua and I wanted to have a baby. I must be honest and say that I was fearful of being a mom, of being in charge of another human beings' life and fearful that I would make the same mistakes as my parents. I have realized that once again I must let go and let God. So Joshua and I prayed for strength and wisdom to raise a child, asked the Lord for His hand in the matter and believed for an answer. At five weeks I took a pregnancy test and it was positive. We were so excited but wanted to wait for doctor's confirmation before telling everyone. One morning when I was getting ready for work there was a lot of blood in my urine; I immediately freaked out and broke down crying. I woke up Joshua and told him everything. As we rushed to the doctor, fear and negative thoughts filled my mind. I was afraid I lost the baby, afraid there was something wrong with my body and afraid that I might not be able to have children. The doctor told me I would have to go through three rounds of blood testing and have an early ultrasound. The worst part was that all this occurred over the weekend and the following Monday was Labor Day. We would have to endure more waiting and the fear that we had lost our baby. Even though my emotions were up and down like a roller coaster and I was filled with fear, Joshua decided to trust the Lord. He declared life into my womb and rebuked all fear. A week later we received the good news that we were still pregnant and everything was normal. We are currently awaiting the arrival of our baby boy!

    One thing I have learned is that our fear can paralyze, but faith moves. The Lord's Word holds true, "...if we are faithless, He remains faithful..." 2 Timothy 2:13 ESV. Please learn from my mistakes dear sister, and do not give in to fear. Do not believe the lies from the enemy and do not allow fear to control you. Remember that God's power is greater than your fear. In His Word, He says, "Fear not, for I am with you; be not dismayed, for I am your God. I will strengthen you, Yes, I will help you, I will uphold you with My righteous right hand" Isaiah 41:10 ESV.

    The Lord isn't waiting for you to fail; He's waiting for you to run to Him! Seek His face when you are fearful, in any situation, there is nothing too small or too big. Romans 8:38-39 NASB states, "and I am convinced that nothing can ever separate us from God's love. Neither death nor life, neither angels nor demons, neither our fears for today nor our worries about tomorrow—not even the powers of hell can separate us from God's love. No power in the sky above or in the earth below—indeed, nothing in all creation will ever be able to separate us from the love of God that is revealed in Christ Jesus our Lord."

Here are some verses to meditate on when dealing with fear:

"The Lord is on my side; I will not fear. What can man do to me?" Psalm 118:6 (ESV)

"Peace I leave with you; my peace I give to you. Not as the world gives do I give to you. Let not your hearts be troubled, neither let them be afraid." John 14:27 (ESV)

"For you did not receive the spirit of slavery to fall back into fear, but you have received the Spirit of adoption as sons, by whom we cry, "Abba, Father." Romans 8:15 (ESV)

"For God has not given us a spirit of fear, but of power and love and self-control." 2 Timothy 1:7 (ESV)

Let's Pray

Heavenly Father I lift up my sister to you now and any fear that she may feel. I ask that your Holy Spirit would overwhelm her and that she would feel your peace that surpasses all understanding. Thank you, Father, that you are faithful even when we are fearful. I pray that you would give her discernment over the lies of the enemy and that she would rebuke them before they even find footing. I ask that your Word becomes so deeply rooted in her that she is not swayed one way or another. Thank you, Father, for her sound mind and for the clarity to keep pushing forward. I ask all of these things in Jesus name, Amen!

The Sixth Love Language

God is my love language. He is constantly talking to me about His love, different ways he reveals it to me, and ways I can better love others and how much he loves me. Here's a letter from Him to us:

My Child,
You've had it wrong,
all along,
but here
allow me to lift your mind,
shine, polish and make it new.

Love, distorted--is not what you've made it; it rages against the thought of being a sudden temporary mist.
Kissed by the lips of my Father, it is not an emotion;
nor is it a feeling.

Love is the agreeing promise of a mind and heart saying "I commit to you. Through the fleeting beauty, faulty feelings and hazardous emotions reeling in your life."

Love is, the sacrificial action; showing one that I will bleed for you, plead for you to be forgiven as I continue to take on lashings because I've committed myself to see you live.
It is the conscious choice to rescue one's heart from the plague of sin,
rather than pretend,
allowing the greed of selfish ambition to suffocate current progress and irresponsibly disappoint

Rise Up to Greatness

Love is, the indulgence of another being;
an indulgence overwhelmingly satisfying, due to the fact it will never truly be satisfied.
But still, you've tried and tried,
and you'll try and try, to fill that appetite with empty calories.
But Child, it can never be satisfied.
-You'll always want and need more.
It is the unified cord tunneling power to your heart monitor,
allowing a constant beep. beep. beep. to ring in your ears,
promising to never be unplugged.

Love is, more entanglement than a four letter word has the strength or willingness to hold.
And so I promise,
I've committed to you through the fleeting beauty, faulty feelings and hazardous emotions reeling in your life.
I have already shown you that I will bleed for you,
plead for you to be forgiven
and continue to take on lashings
because I've committed myself to see you live.
I choose to provide rescue
rather than to allow selfish ambition to suffocate our current progress.
I find rest in filling pages of a mental notebook solely based on you
not that I need to;
I could never forget.
I indulged in you before you knew me;
I abandoned myself to you.
And though your indulgence of me can never be satisfied,
I grant you satisfaction with the fact that there's no end to me and always more to learn,
and yearn for.
I promise to never unplug the monitor to your heart
no matter how many months you've been in the coma.

I have promised to be devoted to every single thing you are, and I love you with all of the entanglement *I* have the strength and the willingness to hold.
Love,
Jesus

1 John 4:10 "This is love: not that we loved God, but that he loved us and sent his Son as an atoning sacrifice for our sins."

Let's Pray
Your love stretches far beyond my understanding. I am constantly overwhelmed by the depths of your love. Who am I that you love me with a love so pure? I will never understand it, but I am so grateful. Thank you for who you are and thank you for your love! You sent your only Son as an atoning sacrifice for MY sins, and still, you love me even when I turn my back on you. You love me when I sin against you, and when I do not trust you. You love me when I place lies over your truth. Jesus, please help me to better love and trust you. Your love is the one thing that can satisfy my soul, and even then I want more and more. Thank you that I don't have to work for your love, but it's freely given. Thank you for loving me through and through. There is nothing that can separate me from your love and I want to dwell in it forever. Help me, Lord. Help me to better love others. I want to see and love them as you do. I put down my own selfish ambition so that I may love as you want me to. Your love is greater than anything this world has to offer, and I want to offer it to every person I meet. Grow that in me as I grow in you. Thank you, I love you. Amen.

Pain

"Find a place inside where there's joy, and the joy will burn out the pain."
–Joseph Campbell

Losing Someone Special

"And God will wipe away every tear from their eyes; there shall be no more death nor sorrow, nor crying. There shall be no more pain for the former things have passed way." Revelation 21:4 (NKJV)

The dreaded day came on Saturday, June 19, 1971, when my mother succumbed to cancer. Her name was Nayda Plaza-Colon. She was 35 years old at the time of her death. As many others, I have experienced tremendous losses, dark moments, painful experiences, health issues and financial crisis. However, losing my mother has been the greatest loss of my life. Her death was the most devastating trial to endure. No 11 year old should grow up without her or his mom. On that morbid Saturday, so many years ago, part of me died with my mother. A part that only the Lord could revive and He most certainly did.

The Lord has sent many "mothers" in the course of my life, which I am deeply grateful. Yet, no one quite loved me the way she did. Her love was special. Truly, the Lord has been faithful. His comfort and compassion saw me through every stage of my life.
In essence, she was my first friend. Trust builds a friendship. Trust is the bridge that unites two hearts and makes them one. No one is able to be a true friend without trusting the other person. The challenge is whether to trust or not to trust, especially if you know the pain of betrayal. I trusted my mother with all my heart. My life was safe in her hands. There was no doubt that her love, devotion, care, and support were genuine. As a young child, I believed that I was a superstar. Actually, I had a superstar for a mother.

By modern society standards, my mother was poor. For a poor woman, she left a rich legacy to love and serve God with all my soul, heart and mind. Real living is loving and serving the Lord, which will satisfy the deep crevices of your soul. If you love God, I mean truly love Him, you will love people. Our daily interaction with family, co-workers, friends, and neighbors is to show God's love. We are to love and treat people with dignity and respect. Do not complain when times are difficult but trust that God knows what He is doing. Be quick to forgive or bitterness will destroy you from the person that God has intended you to be. She penned in my heart this "unwritten will".

The 'Rose' was my mother's favorite flower. The day of her burial, my brothers and sister decided to place a rose in her hands. In our innocence, to make sure that the day we went to heaven we could identify our mother. I miss you mom but one day I will see you in heaven. God's grace brought me comfort. Only His grace healed the little girl's, broken heart.

Perhaps, today your heart is broken. You have lost a special person in your life. Whether you're young or old, losing a loved one is never easy. In essence part of you dies with the person because they are irreplaceable. Their absence has left a huge void in your heart. A deep sorrow has settled in your soul. The Lord is near the brokenhearted and He is near you. Jesus is weeping with you. He understands your pain. He will comfort you each and every passing moment when your sorrow is unbearable.

Let's Pray
Father, for every grieving person, I ask that you send the comfort of your Holy Spirit. You are the only one that truly understands the depth of their pain. Abba God be the lifter of their heads, give them the strength that they will need today. We thank you for your grace, in Jesus' name. Amen

It's Going To Be Okay

So what does a 40-year-old woman have in common with a teenage girl? The fact that we are both females might be the only thing. Do you agree? Honestly, there is so much more. For instance, if you were anything like me growing up, everything felt like it was the end of the world. If your best friend was hanging out with someone else, friendship over. If you forgot a homework assignment and a notice went to your parents, life over! And who could forget the boy you were going to marry just broke up with you. For the love of God kill me now! Sound familiar?

Trust me those feelings are all too real. The ideas of someone rejecting you or you disappointing someone you care deeply about are real feelings. What is not real is your life being over. Let me fill you in on something; no matter how bad you think it's going to get, it is better to let someone know what is happening so that you don't make choices that can alter the course of your life. The statement that says, the truth shall set you free, works. I see too many kids getting into worse trouble just because they were afraid their parents would find out the truth. Sometimes those choices are more devastating than having done the right thing at the right time.

Growing up I never drank or did drugs; it just wasn't my thing. I wanted to be in control of whatever situation I put myself in and actually would end up being the mother hen to everyone else who decided it was what they wanted to do. That by no means made me perfect. I had other issues I had to deal with and well at 16 I became a mother. However, I made a choice that I would live to regret to this day and it was made out of fear. So much fear and I would never understand the repercussions or the effect it would have on my life. If I would've spoken to someone or had the courage to say what was going on I wouldn't have carried the weight or burden of a decision that would forever change my mind and heart. Before my son, I was pregnant and out of fear I made the choice to have an abortion. My life was never the same. I was terrified but my fear was nothing compared to what I felt after it happened. I became cold and callous, not to mention, at the time it happened, the father never knew. I know the Lord forgives and forgets, and I am thankful for His grace but I wish I could forget too.

When I became pregnant the second time, I was so worried about what my family might say or feel. However, this time in my mind I thought I was correcting the wrong I had done, by having the baby. The one thing I never considered was the kind of life my son might have. We never think beyond a moment, we only try to live in it while never considering repercussions, but only what will satisfy our current situation. Never thinking how far did I go and how deeply have I hurt others? I know I disappointed my family, I was young and they were worried. Just like any loving family, you worry. And to me, it seemed like the end of the world. However, I was wrong and it was the beginning of something beautiful for me. Now I am not encouraging teen pregnancy with the previous statements. Remember there are repercussions to being a teen mom and most of it affects the child, not you. Having my son stopped me from making some very poor choices and I wanted to be the person he looked up to when he thought about being a better person or success. I was terribly behind in school. If I remember correctly, I think I needed 18 credits to graduate but I had about 12. In one year I managed to obtain all the credits necessary to graduate by going to school during the day and night while holding a part time job. It wasn't easy, and thankfully my family supported me. I made a choice to ensure I had all the necessary skills to finish my education and obtain a job. The bright side of that was getting home those late nights and my baby boy being awake waiting for kisses and hugs from his mom. There were moments I did feel judgment from others who possibly expected me to fail. Perhaps they even wanted me to fail. Maybe I was exactly what they expected of me. A young Latina girl who would be a teen mom was destined to live her life working on public assistance or working two jobs. That judgment was heavy, but it wasn't the end of the world. It was other people's thoughts of me but not my thoughts of who I was and what I was to become. I will never forget that year, for the moments of tears,

there were moments filled with laughter and love. It was not the end of my world but only the beginning of a not so perfect life, however, filled with perfect love. I am reminded of this scripture when I think about this time in my life:
John 16:33 "I have told you all this so that you may have peace in me. Here on earth, you will have many trials and sorrows. But take heart, because I have overcome the world."

He has overcome the world so whatever I am going through is not the end of my world.

Let's Pray
Father, thank you for overcoming the world so that I might have hope in you knowing that no matter how terrible the trial, how difficult the walk you are standing with me. I ask you to speak this very word into the heart of my sister reading this right now. Remind her of your unfailing love, your unfailing truth, and your wisdom to overcome every situation in her life. The road can be lonely at times, but if we take the time to talk to you and listen silently to hear your voice, we will know what we're going through can never compare to the ultimate sacrifice you gave for our lives. You overcame the world so we can overcome each and every trial that we have and will face. There is a victory in you. Eternal victory in our King! In Jesus name I thank you for the reminder it is going to be okay.

Get Up...Enough is Enough!

John 5: 8-9 Then Jesus," said to him, "Get up! Pick up your mat and walk." At once the man was cured; he picked up his mat and walked. (NIV)

I was the runt of my mother's brood; there were six of us. My mother did the best that she could, considering my father traveled a lot. However, she had us very well trained, like little ducklings all in a row. There were days when the house would get unruly and I would always find myself at the bottom of a wrestling pile of arms, legs, and torsos. I never seemed to be able to take up for myself. I was always in a headlock or full Nelson, a classic wrestling move, screaming, "Get up, let me go", but to no avail. I guess I was an easy target even back then because with all the ruckus in the house I was never ever really heard. I remember once when my sister decided to grow fingernails and tried them out on my face, I didn't cry out loud or defend myself. But my mom saw my bloody tears running down my face from across the room. She grabbed my sister's hand and a nail clipper and chopped them off right then, very firmly saying, "You will not grow nails in this house and use them as a weapon!" I think she might have realized what my temperament was that day, and the enemy relied on the assaults against my body from then on. Not having the physical strength or mental drive or the "chutzpah", a word used in the Jewish culture for nerve or audacity, to say or do anything to defend myself. I was the proverbial sheep going to the slaughterhouse. This went on throughout my life, from childhood to adulthood, in school and on my jobs.

There are several spirits that are released over you at an early age when there is trauma involved in your upbringing. Some of the spirits assigned to me were fear and intimidation, which are attached to their cousin's deaf and dumb spirits. These groups of spirits rely on you first to be afraid, I mean afraid of EVERYTHING! Then you are afraid of people and you become intimidated. A better explanation is that the fear of people rejecting you is now your normal behavior. Which now invites the cousin's deaf and dumb spirits to join in and these two keep your mouth shut so you can't speak out or up for yourself. You are gagged from the inside out and the voice of the Holy Spirit isn't clear anymore, so you listen to your own advice and not His. The combination described was a deadly mix and an open door for many traumatic episodes that tormented me almost my entire life. One incident after the other, like a stairway, each step took me further away from the destiny that God had for me. And the sad part was that I was not aware I had been targeted and the things that were happening to me were not a coincidence, but intentional assaults. Satan used people in my life to wear me down and drown out my voice.

One summer when I was in my teens, I went on a family vacation with a friend. Innocent enough we did what teens do, shopping, talking, walking the neighborhood, and seeing all her old friends. We were invited to the community center's summer teen dance. I'll never forget it; my heart was already racing just by the invitation because I was a far cry from a party doll. I don't think I'd gone to a party outside of my local school's holiday dances that were held in the cafeteria. So, we got dressed and I was so excited because I didn't know what to expect, nor did I know these people but she did, they were old friends and family she said. We dressed to go and it was very crowded, this event was the biggest thing going on in this small town on a Saturday evening.

Once we arrive, my friend immediately leaves me by myself to dance and socialize with her friends. At this time in my life, I am very fearful of being by myself so my excitement has now turned into fear. One song, two songs, and then several songs and I eventually lose sight of her in the crowd. That's when it happened!
This entire time one of her friends had been watching me, taking in my body language, facial expressions, just watching, and waiting for the right moment to pounce. He asks me to dance and I say no, I'm okay, and he just takes my hand and continues to coax me to the dance floor. It was already a tight squeeze and I look up and there is my friend giving me the thumbs up to dance with her friend, I believed her that he was safe. Like a sheep to slaughter I do, one

song, then two songs then the dreaded slow song. The boy takes my body close to his and begins to grope me. I was shocked, afraid, and ashamed all at the same time. I didn't see her anymore, my face was screaming stop, but my mouth hasn't said a word. We were crammed in on the dance floor so my wiggling just made it worse. I was trapped! I took it, all of it until I felt like I would throw up. The song finally ended he took me back to where I was standing and left me. As tears filled my eyes I still couldn't find my friend. I tried to hold it in but I couldn't and ran outside for air. While outside, a few people asked if I was okay. I said yes, but became a little overwhelmed by the crowd. I told them I was there with my friend; they knew her and said they would go get her for me. One guy did but the other stayed outside with me making small talk until I guess I "looked" ok. He probably could tell how uneasy I was but he didn't try anything, he just kept talking. That night led to other episodes of physical and emotional attacks on my body, where my gagged tongue just let it happen.

Another time when I was in high school and one of my best friends was dating a football player. They decided to go hang out in a relative's empty house and invited me and several other girls to go with them. Dumb me never saw the set up coming. We all get to the house and there were several other football players there and boy they were glad to see us. I didn't think too much of it since we were in a group. But then it happened; one couple decides to go to one of the bedrooms. This action was the clue for the other guys to pick a girl and take her to the other rooms in the house. I wasn't cool with it at all, but I wasn't going to be the first to say anything. So, I didn't and not saying anything was telling him yes. Never being exposed to this type of situation, I thought maybe we would go into the room and talk, cause I kind of liked him, and maybe he knew I did and this was going to be like a first date. I said all that to make this be okay in my head, to calm me down. I wasn't sure what he was thinking but it was NOT what I was thinking. We ended up in a small bedroom where the furniture was very tight fitting. We sat on the edge of the bed and I thought it was nice; we're going to talk. But we didn't and the moment quickly turned. I was so

Rise Up to Greatness

inexperienced; I didn't have a clue as to what was going to happen next. Now I know today it would have been called date rape.

He began to kiss me, harder and harder until he had full control of me. He managed to push me on the bed and roll on top of me. He was very experienced, I could tell. He began to grope me all over while he was pinning me down to the bed. By now my mind is in full scream mode. NO!! NO!!! This can NOT be happening to me! I'm a virgin! I'm supposed to wait until I'm married! I heard my parent's voices, each taking turns on what good girls do and wait until you're married. It was like my life was flashing before my eyes and as fast as my mind was going was just as fast as he was going on top of me. How did I get to this place, what did I do to ask for this? Was it because I liked him and I didn't say no? This is NOT what I wanted!

By now we are rolling on the bed and I realized I need to keep my wits about me. I needed to fight! Mind you I've not said ONE word, not one blessed word!! But in my head, I'm in an all-out war!! I'm rolling and struggling with this boy who is at least two times my size. Somehow in all the rolling he had taken off my sweater and is now trying to unzip my pants. Survivor mode kicked in and Thank God for turtle neck shirts! I had tucked mine in my pants and the war to try and pull the shirt out of my jeans had begun. And yet, I hadn't said one word. What so crazy is, I'm not sure if I did if he would've stopped. That might have been normal behavior for him, I just didn't know anymore. The boy was like two octopuses, arms and legs, and strong. Now he has my shirt out of my pants and over my breast. But that darn turtle neck stopped right at my neck. Now he's groping my breast and pulling on my pants at the same time. At this point, it was serious and I didn't know what to do. There was no one in that room to pull him off me like my mother pulled my sister when she scratched my face. When the first assault to my body began, it came to me, call on Jesus. Yes, call on Jesus!! So, in my head, not my mouth, I began to say very softly Jesus, Jesus, Jesus. Then I began to scream His powerful and precious name JESUS!!! And at that moment one of the other girls screamed from the other room, you could hear her and the boy yelling and scuffling. It wasn't just me not wanting to be there and that gave me strength and it jarred him too. I cannot tell you what happened next because I don't remember, but I do remember him pushing me, like throwing my body on the bed and him getting up, frustrated and leaving me in the room. I laid there for a moment pulling my clothes and myself together. Holding on, fighting back the tears, leaving that room and going to the living room and just waiting on the sofa until the rest of the crew made it in. I still didn't scream take me home right now, I just couldn't. But my friend, who was screaming, screamed it for me, Thank God!

I never told anyone what happened because we didn't know what date rape was back then. Those spirits set me up to be a target that night. It took many years and many times of assault on my person before I realized the spirit of assault was released over my life.

Years later I was in a church that offered a congregational deliverance service where they ask you a series of questions and as the Holy Spirit reveals it to you by the spirit, you're free to release it. This was the beginning of my journey to finding my voice. If any of these stories sounds like you, then be encouraged, there is hope! There are many ways to find your voice. I took a long way around but you don't have to. Pray and ask the Holy Spirit to reveal to you anything in your past that could have been an open door to these spirits. Then renounce them, forgive yourself, these acts were not your fault. The enemy would like to deceive you into believing you had something to do with these things happening to you, but he is a liar! That spirit is a predatory spirit and it will draw you out without you having to do anything.

Like David and Bathsheba, David had a sexual sin issue and because he wasn't whole he saw an opportunity to take advantage of a woman who was not his. His spirit of sexual brokenness drove him to abuse Bathsheba. David, like so many of our abusers, had been abused as well. These spirits were released over them to torment them to act out. When they put their hands on us they were acting out from their own pain that hasn't been given over to God. All of God's children are victims of these vicious spirits.

These series of events are what the enemy hopes will shut our voices down, but we must push past our feelings and see that the Lord has so much more for us. Recognize how this set up was used to hinder our growth in the Kingdom. When these things happen, we as women must realize that it wasn't us but the spirit against us that has altered our emotional and sometimes physical growth. Reader, if anything that I have shared has happened to you, Shake yourself!! Dig in deep to find a place of healing and wholeness! Don't let your trauma paralyze you! You have something to say! You have someone's healing in your mouth. They're waiting for you to tell your story, to give counsel and wisdom; To love them, because they feel unloved. I said to myself GET UP!! ENOUGH IS ENOUGH!! Get up, stop the pain and move in the direction of your purpose and destiny.

Let's Pray
Father in the name of Jesus, I thank you for the woman who is strong enough to take the brunt of this thing called life. I believe when she was formed before the foundation of the world you already knew what road she would take and what would happen to her. In your kindness, you expanded her heart to embrace forgiveness, courage, and grace to do the hard thing. To forgive, let go and release those who she might be holding unforgiveness for in her heart. God, I believe like the man at the pool of Bethesda, she is taking up her bed and walking, walking towards her healing, walking towards her destiny, walking towards her future as a daughter of the Most High God! Continue to lead, guide and direct her Lord Jesus, hold her head up, keep her heart true to the things of God and use her mightily in this culture as a voice to the hurting and abused. In the Precious Name of Jesus, Amen.

Salty

"And he said, "Bring me a new bowl, and put salt in it." So they brought it to him. Then he went out to the source of the water, and cast in the salt there, and said, "Thus says the LORD: 'I have healed this water; from it, there shall be no more death or barrenness.' " II Kings 2:20-21 (NKJV)

When restaurants are marketing new additions to their menus, they sometimes use the term "bold flavor". A restaurant chain house might use the phrase to describe a new dish or signature beverage. This term is used because **bold** means intense, distinct, stands out. So of course if these companies want to grab our attention and get us to buy their new product, they will tell us that the item is different than what you've had before. It stands out and that the flavor is deliciously intense! My question to you is this: If God were to try marketing us, his daughters and sons, would he be able to say that we have bold flavor and are seasoned with salt?
You might be asking yourself, "How can Believers have flavor, let alone BOLD flavor?" Well, the word says that we are the salt of the earth. Salt has many uses, but the most common use is to enhance flavor. This metaphor was used in the Bible to let the disciples know that they were responsible for "flavoring" the world with the knowledge and wisdom, or the gospel that Christ had taught them. We are modern day followers of Christ, thus we are charged with doing the same thing. So, the Bible tells us that we have to be salty, but it does not give specifics concerning how we gain our saltiness; God chooses the life experiences we have to get us where we need to be.

Salt is also used as a healing agent. Salt has been used for centuries to treat various ailments by increasing circulation in the body and decreasing water retention, among other things. Knowing that salt not only adds flavor but also has healing qualities, I've concluded that some of the experiences I've had in the past were so that I could help usher someone into their healing in the future. God said that I have to be salty and ***I had no choice*** in how He made me that way.

Roughly 1 in 4 women on college campuses (staggering statistics, I know) are sexually assaulted. I was sexually assaulted during my senior year of college. I struggled with it, not knowing how to seek help for the emotional pain I was carrying and not trusting myself enough to know if it was really sexual assault. I didn't know what to call what happened to me because I blamed myself. As a result, I remained silent for quite a while. When I did muster up the courage to speak up, my experiences were minimized because people struggled to understand something that I couldn't even understand. How could I expect them to sympathize when I didn't even know what to call what happened to me? To use a colloquialism, I was SALTY! I was annoyed that he did it and that it caused me so much pain. I was frustrated that seemingly no one understood. I became resentful about something that God actually intended to use for healing. God put me in a situation that made me salty so that I could use that salt to help others heal.

A lot of the work I do is with survivors of trauma, specifically sexual trauma. I have been working with this population for much of my clinical career and it wasn't until recently I realized it was not an accident. I wondered why client after client assigned to me had a history of sexual trauma. At first, I was scared because I didn't want my past to affect my work with my clients. I've worked with women who blamed themselves just like I did. I've worked with men who were too embarrassed to seek help for fear of being marginalized. With my clinical knowledge and personal experience, I have been able to help them through and see things from a different perspective; to see their own value, not based solely on book knowledge, but self-knowledge. So what I went through gave me a testimony, but more importantly, it's a testimony that helps me to help others see their own testimony.

Let's Pray

Father God, thank you for your word that says we overcome by the word or our testimony. Thank you for the tests that give us testimonies because they strengthen us and help us to strengthen others. Lord, I ask that you give us a faith that is bold enough to heal situations. I pray that the light, the salt, and the God that is in us, is used to touch others and mend broken pieces. Thank you, Lord, for using what we thought might kill us for our good and the good of others. In Jesus' name, Amen.

Suffering

"Consider it all joy, my brethren, when you encounter trials, knowing that the testing of your faith produces endurance. And let endurance have its perfect work, that you may be perfect and complete, lacking nothing." James 1:2-4 (NASB)

Suffering, trials, and tribulations, at some point or another we will experience them. Whether it's the death of a loved one, end of a relationship, loss of job or persecution for your faith, the list can go on. We know it all too well.
Neither my family nor I have been exempt from such suffering and trials. We all have a story and I would like to share a personal story with you. I'm not sure if my mom ever knew this, but she is my hero. She has faced countless trials and experienced much suffering. In 1967 my mom lost her mother at age 18 and was left to survive on her own. 10 years later in 1977, she decided to move to Texas to start a new life, not knowing anyone. In 1981 she married and the next year had a son named Jerrod. Within six months of his birth, she knew something was different about her baby boy. She soon learned he had cerebral palsy and permanent brain damage. He would never be able to walk or talk. In the same year, her husband was later killed in a plane crash. She carried on.

She met my father in 1983 and three years later she gave birth to me in 1986; my parents married May of 1988. My mom knew about the Lord, and had been searching for him, but didn't start walking with Him until participating in a Bible study class in 1988. She was growing in the Lord and all was well until a summer vacation in 1993; my dad had a sudden heart attack and passed away. Another devastating loss and the pain, excruciating! Not wanting to blame God, but she was angry, hurting and crying out why Lord, why? Now she was left to raise two small children, one having special needs. I was six years old at the time and Jerrod was eleven. She did the only thing she knew to do and that was to carry on. She trusted the Lord and continued her life. Of course, desiring not to be alone and wanting a complete family for her children, she started dating again in 1994.

She was remarried in 1997 and prayerfully for the last time. This marriage seemed to be like most, the normal ups and downs that come along with a blended family. However, slowly the micromanaging, anger, jealousy and verbal abuse began and no one was safe from it. Not wanting a divorce and for the love of the man she married, she decided to push through it. Crying out to our Father in Heaven was the only thing my mother and I could do. Time passed and in 2006 when I was old enough and self-sufficient, I left home. I explained to my mom that I couldn't take the abuse anymore and neither should she. Life continued and nothing much changed back at home.

In May 2011, I graduated from college and was thankful I got to see my brother and my mom at that time for we lived hours apart. Little did we know to cherish such time together. My brothers 29th birthday came quickly in June. My mom had some cake for my brother one evening and was trying to get him to open gifts when she could tell something was wrong. He looked tired and completely out of it. It was then when he took one last breath and went home to be in the arms of Jesus. The pain was overwhelming and tears were endless. I couldn't imagine how much more of the pain my mother was experiencing since this was her son, her first born, her baby boy. Even in the midst of this suffering my mom never turned her back on God, never blamed Him, and only continued to trust. As believers, we both knew that Jerrod was now whole, walking and talking with Jesus and that we would see Him again someday. My mom informed me later that at one point when she was crying out to God she said, "Why, Lord, why my only son, I'm in so much pain?" She said God immediately answered with a verse from his Word, "For God so loved the world, that he gave his only Son, that whoever believes in him should not perish but have eternal life." My mom then knew that God understood and saw her pain. She felt encouraged and continued to seek His face.

I'm not going to lie and say that the pain of all these sufferings and trials that my mom or myself have experienced has gone away.

It becomes something that we have to take to the foot of the cross daily and say, Lord, I can't do this or handle this, but I know You can. When you know and trust the Creator of the Universe, that He loves you and has a plan for you even in such pain, He gives you the strength to keep going. We have to remember there is a purpose in our suffering. Some may realize it right away, some of us it comes later down the road and then for others, as with myself, we may never know until we reach Heaven.

Sufferings and trials are all part of life. If you stop and think about it most people in the Bible faced trials, suffered and were tested. Think about the book of Ruth in the Bible where she faced the loss of her husband and then had to decide between going back to her own people to start again or to go with her mother-in-law Naomi, to her homeland. Everything she knew and was comfortable with was gone. Yet she didn't give up and she said to Naomi in Ruth 1:16 NASB, "Don't ask me to leave you and turn back. Wherever you go, I will go; wherever you live, I will live. Your people will be my people, and your God will be my God."

Then there is the story of Esther. Esther became Queen and soon found herself with a huge weight on her shoulders. She had to save her people, the Jews, from death at the hands of Haman. In Esther 4:14 NLT, her uncle Mordecai said, "If you keep quiet at a time like this, deliverance and relief for the Jews will arise from some other place, but you and your relatives will die. Who knows if perhaps you were made queen for just such a time as this?" No pressure right!?

Let us not forget one of the most important people of the Bible, Jesus. He was tempted in Matthew 4:1-11, He experienced loss and abandonment from friends and family members, Mark 3:21 and Mark 14:50. Then there is one of the most important happenings of all and one account is in the entire chapter of Luke 23; Jesus was mocked, beaten and crucified. He suffered for us because He loves us so much.

As hard as it may be to believe, there's value and purpose in our suffering. You may have heard something like this before, but think about a goldsmith or silversmith and the refining of those precious metals. Gold and silver both start out impure and must be placed in the center of the flames and extreme heat to be purified.

The goldsmith or silversmith will remove the precious metal, shape it and return it to the heat, all the while never taking his eyes off of the process. The only way in which he knows that the process is complete is when the metal is shining brightly and he can see his own reflection in it!

Whatever you are going through or whatever you have gone through, know you're not alone. The Lord is watching over you and He has a plan for your pain. 1 Peter 1:7 NLT says, "These trials will show that your faith is genuine. It is being tested as fire tests and purifies gold—though your faith is far more precious than mere gold. So when your faith remains strong through many trials, it will bring you much praise and glory and honor on the day when Jesus Christ is revealed to the whole world." Through such pain and trials, He is strengthening your faith and bringing all the praise and glory to Himself. Don't give up dear sister, "...in the world you will have tribulation. But take heart; I have overcome the world" John 16:33 ESV. In Him, we find our strength and when you call on Him he will hear you and sustain you.

Here are some verses to meditate on:

"Not only that, but we rejoice in our sufferings, knowing that suffering produces endurance, and endurance produces character, and character produces hope." Romans 5:3-4 (ESV)

"And we know that for those who love God all things work together for good, for those who are called according to his purpose." Romans 8:28 (ESV)

"May the God of hope fill you with all joy and peace in believing, so that by the power of the Holy Spirit you may abound in hope." Romans 15:13 (ESV)

"Blessed be the God and Father of our Lord Jesus Christ, the Father of mercies and God of all comfort, who comforts us in all our affliction, so that we may be able to comfort those who are in any affliction, with the comfort with which we ourselves are comforted by God." 2 Corinthians 1:3-4 (ESV)

"My grace is sufficient for you, for my power is made perfect in weakness." 2 Corinthians 12:9 (ESV)

"I will never leave you nor forsake you." Hebrews 13:5 (ESV)

"And after you have suffered a little while, the God of all grace, who has called you to his eternal glory in Christ, will himself restore, confirm, strengthen and establish you." 1 Peter 5:10 (ESV)

<u>Let's Pray</u>
Lord, I thank you that through our suffering You have a plan and a purpose. I ask that You would give my sister your strength and fill her with your Holy Spirit to comfort her in times of pain. I ask that she finds shelter in your Word and comes to feel your sweet presence. Lord, I pray that not only during the hard times but at all times, that she would trust You and seek after you daily. Thank you for the work You are doing in her and the refining process. I pray many blessings over my sister, as well as, your love and protection. I ask all these things in Jesus name, Amen!

It Is Possible

One day as I sat in my favorite chair in the house looking out my back window that overlooked my back porch, I stared out over the trees and green grass that surrounded me. The scenery was beautiful but inside my mind, it was a different story. I thought of all that was coming up in my life. I was excited and worried at the same time. And in that moment I experienced the same emotions I've felt in more difficult times. Suddenly, fear had crept up once again and then I whispered the words, "I don't know if I can do this." "Do I have what it takes?" I think we have all questioned like this a time or two. When we get the opportunity we really wanted or when we hear the news we never saw coming. When life suddenly throws a challenge our way or in my case many challenges, we may say:

- I don't know if I have the strength.
- I don't know if I have the perseverance.
- I don't know if I have the wisdom.
- I don't know if I'm enough.

My life was feeling impossible to me. Have you ever felt that way? Thankfully, when Jesus said we could do all things through Him it included the right now. On our greatest and toughest days, this is something we all long to know, even if we never put it into words. Begin to imagine what you'd look like in the hands of God, protected, loved, accepted and transformed.

I'm a construction worker of sorts, I build walls, the kind that shut people out and protects me from hurt, well, so I thought. I felt safe behind my walls. I'm not proud of these barriers I set up for myself but I've had them for so long they have become a part of me. I guard my heart ever so carefully, I can build a wall never to be taken down and it's always been my safe place. However, for every time I had built a wall or I guarded my heart instead of letting God protect me, I learned that I don't heal and those walls don't break very easily. I've now chosen to trust God to heal and know that He is my safe place, and so should you. When He heals our broken crushed hearts we can breathe again, it's like a breath of fresh air, and we can move past that pain and forgive.

We all have prayed for Gods guidance and protection of our loved ones all their lives but we don't trust Him with our pain? With our hearts? With our brokenness? That must change. Jesus is not afraid of our brokenness, open those doors, throw open those windows and let His light shine in, move those walls that are so carefully guarding your crushed spirit and stop controlling your pain and let God carry that for you, heal you and mend your broken heart. He has said in His Word that He loves us and He meant every word. God is our safe place to hide; ready to help when we need him. Those walls I had so carefully built throughout my life are beginning to come down. Silence is a wall I feel protected in, but if I continue to remain silent then the things God has given me to share will never be shared by anyone else at least, not in the way I would share them. Your life is not impossible to Him.

We are unique individuals created for a purpose of spreading God's love, mercy, forgiveness, and grace in a way that only each of us can in how God has created each and every one of us. Fear doesn't have to remain with us for we can and should give any and all of them to Him. Reader, no matter what you're facing or what fear comes to your thoughts and heart, the same is true for all of us. When that fear comes we can pause and say, yes I have what it takes because I belong to the God who gives all I need and more.

Keep this in mind. The only thing standing in your way of the nothing is impossible life... is you! What do I mean by that? Your thoughts, your past and what you haven't forgiven yourself for, you have heard many times to leave your past right there in the past, but if you haven't, then it's in the way of your nothing is impossible life. And what about the people who hurt you that you will never get an apology from, how much longer are you going to hang on to all that? Forgive them; give them to God because there is nothing we can do about those people. What about family, you know, the ones who shut you out, the ones who have been hateful, unloving, and not accepting of you? Let them go! Give those hurts, those constant thoughts about them, and the guilt that isn't yours to carry, to God. There is no chance at all if you think you can pull it off yourself, but every chance in the world if you trust God to do it.

In the stillness of my home sitting in my favorite chair, it was as though God whispered to my inner being, "What matters isn't if you have what it takes, the question and what matters most is, "will you have what needs to be given?" You will; because God will provide it, this is it. This is what can and will empower you on the days when you feel overwhelmed and defeated. It's the truth you can hold on to when you get discouraged, the wild mystery that lifts life's weight from our shoulders. Nothing is impossible for God, which means with Him, nothing is impossible for us too.

Jesus looked at them and said, "With man this is impossible, but with God all things are possible." Matthew 19:26

Let's Pray
Father, I pray for hearts to be mended and lives to be changed through you. Break those walls that keep us from moving forward in our lives. You Father are our healer, not only to our physical body but for all that is within us and we thank you for that. I pray Father that those who read this can now move forward in their purpose and calling you have for each and every one of these unique and beautiful women. But most of all thank you for loving us and showing us the possible in what we feel is impossible in our lives. Amen

Conquering Loneliness

About halfway through my fifth semester of college, I had been suffering from the feeling of loneliness, which pushed me into a mild depression, causing me to dread even waking up in the morning, or even worse: facing the *entire* day. I felt as if I had no one I could turn to, fellowship with, laugh with or even just live life with, and although it was a lie, it radiated louder than all of the voices of people telling me they loved me. And each time the dark cloud would envelop me; God was sitting there eagerly promising, "Rikeisha, I am here. I have not left you. Please talk to me! Please..." I will admit it was in those moments I would turn to God last. The feeling of loneliness would begin to set in and I would scramble about, reaching out to as many people as I could. It wasn't until after failure, I would cry out to God. I remember the first time I realized this. He simply questioned back to me, "Rikeisha. Why am I always your last option?" That question in itself was enough to break a heart, and that was when I realized I had been trying to conquer the loneliness in my own strength and with my own understanding. I was going to God last when I should've gone to him first since He is the only one that could supply all of my needs. The Lord helped me to conquer that dark time by reminding me that He was always with me, and by constantly showing me people he had intentionally given me. It wasn't something I automatically conquered, of course. It was a process and is still something I have to fight against to this day.

I have to constantly remind myself I'm not alone and that I have the power and authority to tell satan he is a liar for trying to convince me that I am. It is so easy for us to believe a lie over truth, and though it doesn't make sense, we easily fall into the trap of deceit. However, the incredible thing is what God says really is true! If you have or are experiencing those feelings of loneliness, He says he will never leave or forsake us and we're not alone. The Lord puts our names in people's hearts so they can either pray for us or reach out to us. He doesn't miss a thing, and his heart breaks as we place what the enemy says over what He says. He understands though and still, he doesn't leave us.

Isaiah 41:10 "So do not fear, for <u>I am with you</u>; do not be dismayed, for I am your God. I will strengthen you and help you; I will uphold you with my righteous right hand."

<u>Let's Pray</u>
Lord, thank you for always being with me. Thank you for never leaving me or forsaking me. I thank you that your word is true and no lie from the enemy is above it. I promise to go to you first whenever I start to feel as if I am completely alone. Please equip me with the knowledge and wisdom to help others who may be feeling lonely. I know in doing that, the enemy's plan will completely backfire. I promise to lay the feelings of loneliness at the foot of your cross every single day. I give it completely to you, and I receive your presence, knowing that you are always with me. Thank you for all of the people you have placed in my life to remind me that I am not alone. And most of all, thank you for seeing me and understanding why I feel the way I do. You don't miss a single detail, but you still love me with a love unimaginable. You are enough for me, help me to remember that. I love you. Amen.

Spirit

"You have to expect spiritual warfare whenever you stand up for righteousness or call attention to basic values. It's just a matter of light battling the darkness. But the light wins every time. You can't throw enough darkness on light to put it out."
–Thomas Kinkade

He Wants Your Worship!

The enemy is not concerned with your family, your spouse or your children. He could care less about your job; the lovely home you have or your relationships. All he wants to do is cut your worship with your heavenly Father because if He can take your worship, everything else becomes a casualty of war.

One early morning in my car, I was meditating and thinking about making a choice that would alter my life forever. I could not understand it at first. All I remember being taught in church was the enemy was after all those things, everything that is important to me, but when I heard this that day it all made sense. His job is to keep my heart, mind, and spirit focused on everything else but God and if that happens well then, of course, my life would fall apart.

Before I encountered God I was on the verge of divorce; I was almost 20 years old with two children, and my husband was an alcoholic. We weren't happy, always fighting, and dealing with insecurities. My knight's armor had turned dull, and the princess had become a spoiled brat! I remember thinking what am I doing, I have two kids, I am going out of my mind and I can't handle this. I had nowhere to turn, and my friends meant well by giving me the advice to 'let him go' because they knew I was dealing with a lot. I will never forget that I spoke to my mother and told her my plan to live with her until I figured everything out. My fairytale was over! Although I didn't know the Lord the way I know Him now, I managed to pray a prayer that I will never forget.

I asked God to show me how to serve Him and to WORSHIP Him the way He wanted me too. Who says those things? What in the world was I talking about worship?? What is that? A few months later our lives were turned completely upside down because God stepped in. I never would've thought that the basis of that prayer would be the fight I would have during my entire walk in the Lord. Even worse, I did not figure that out until recently.

Rise Up to Greatness

When I talk about worship I'm not talking about your typical Sunday praise sessions. I'm not talking about your times when you may be singing off key in the shower (just me?). I am talking about the time spent alone, face to the ground no one in the room crying out like you are the last person on earth worship sessions.

Keep what you're about to read well noted and hidden deep in your heart. When you set out to get to know God in intimate levels, you're declaring war, and I mean war in your life. It doesn't sound very encouraging, but I promise there is a happy ending. Every time you proclaim His love over someone's life, every time you unashamedly share His gospel, every moment you spend looking to please your Fathers heart, you are at war with the enemy. The best part about that is you are doing it while breathing the very breath of God. When you make those declarations, you're causing discomfort to the enemy's ear, which is like a loud annoying sound to him.

Have you ever noticed when you share or see someone share the gospel and His love in a way that's inviting, it is met with anger? There is something about true worship and in the forms that it comes that drives the enemy mad. The enemy will stop at nothing to get you to stop praying, fasting, seeking God's presence. The enemy will send distractions as you draw closer to the Lord. If you allow the distractions, you'll begin to ignore the very nature of it and fall into the trap of lies. Next thing you know you are in a place you never imagined you would be, making compromises you would have NEVER made in the past.

Your life in the kingdom of God has great power and purpose, but the enemy will fight to keep you from finding out what your power and purpose is.

I never understood believers who went through something traumatic and would attend church the next day. I would think don't you need time for yourself; don't you need to grieve the situation or figure it out? The truth is they were going to a place where a source of hope could be found in connecting with others who would stand in prayer and support to keep them FOCUSED. They understood that no matter the situation, they couldn't lose sight on where their help was. I could never walk away from the Lord, not willingly; He has given much and FORGIVEN much for me. Even as I write, this heart aches to think of the pain I caused others this year and how I broke the heart of my Heavenly Father. Even in the midst of my sin, He was talking to me, saying, Selina, HE WANTS YOUR WORSHIP; the enemy wants every part of you. He wants your thoughts to be somewhere else except on me. If you will believe it, I even heard it verbalized, "I want all of you." If the enemy had my mind he would have my thoughts and then grab hold of my heart to turn it to stone. I've had dreams of fighting an enemy constantly after me. Then I understood it plainly; the enemy has to take me out because to keep me in the battle will mean he can't gain ground. My worship, my adoration, my reverence shifts the atmosphere. It helps me see beyond the natural into the supernatural, and if I see what's there and it is not pleasing unto my Father, I have the authority and ability to change the situation. My worship, our worship can affect, break, change, dominate, liberate, overcome, overtake, rebuild, renew, restore, set, and shift, ANY situation we are facing. Believe me, if it weren't true, the enemy would never come after the very thing that causes God's eye to look upon you.

Deuteronomy 11:16 (NLT) "But be careful. Don't let your heart be deceived so that you turn away from the Lord and serve and worship other gods."

We are dealing with a being that is aware of our carnal tendencies. Stay awake and alert to what is sent your way as a distraction. Can we pray?

Let's Pray
Father, I thank you for giving us the gift to worship freely. I pray that the woman reading this now knows that you are a Father that delights in hearing her voice when she speaks. That her prayers produce ripple effects that cannot be reproduced. I ask that you protect her mind and heart from every attack of the enemy and that she's surrounded by women who will uplift and stand with her in ways she has not experienced before. I pray that she encounters you in ways that keep her in constant desire to please You and to bless your people. Keep her safe, give her rest in the time of battle or

distraction and remind her how much You value her in Jesus name. Amen!

Fight or Die!

1 Corinthians 15:32 "I fought the beast at Ephesus"

For many centuries men would duel with each other to defend their honor, to rectify offenses or to meet challenges. One of the definitions for dueling means "a struggle for domination between two contending persons, groups or ideas." This was a proper way to fight your opponent with a sword or gun.

When the enemy of your soul decides to challenge you for your life... you'd better be prepared to fight and to win. In 1 Corinthians 15:32 Paul says "... I have fought with beasts at Ephesus." That was my victory cry after years of oppression and depression.

I was a very unassuming young lady, small framed and nothing to write home about. I had low self-esteem and was rejected by my male peers for as long as I could remember. Others would compare me to my well-endowed sister as the really thin one, and I heard every thin girl joke to be told. I was introverted, quiet, hardly talked at all and was never able to take up for myself in word or action. I was disliked in college for no apparent reason and gravitated toward jobs where controlling Jezebel spirits were rampant. More often I heard what was wrong with me, not remembering anything being right with me.

The enemy's case against me was set and he went in for the kill. At 17 he sent my first real boyfriend. What a loose term "boyfriend". Yes, they are boys, but not always your friend. Like most women, you give him yourself, your heart, your soul, and just about everything else! And it's funny how it somehow always seems one-sided.

After years of taking me apart, layer by layer, bit by bit and piece by piece, I was beginning to feel the pull of the unraveling. I fell into the deepest pit of despair, a hole so deep you'd never see the bottom or the top of it. And in that hole, is the darkest of dark, the saddest of sad and the loneliness of lonely.

Rise Up to Greatness

All of this was the setup, the case to destroy me; I was helpless to the attacks. They always came from a hand that I knew and was familiar with. In my heart of love, I just couldn't believe that someone could hate me so much and hurt me so deeply. It's the slow fade of the "trust me I have your best interest at heart; Let me do this, let me do that." Then, you are in automatic receive mode. Now you take it sometimes without words being spoken to you because you're now conditioned to take the negative blows, almost like you deserve it. The case is set.

I was far away from the church, God, family, and very isolated. But one day I became aware that every time I drove past this particular church my stomach pulled, not knowing it was the Holy Spirit drawing me to Him, very slowly and so loving. This went on for months and I finally gave in to the gentle nudging. I went and recommitted my life and the slow process of putting "me" back together began.

Now I'm saved, filled with the Holy Spirit, and getting filled with the word. I fell madly in love with my Savior, and Creator. I relocated to another church that flowed more freely in the gifts and the purposes of God. This church had everything: intimate worship, good word, amazing small groups, and mission support. This church grew me spiritually in ways I didn't know existed in the Body of Christ. I was even promoted to home group leader. I led a group of women every other week to the feet of Jesus. But satan had created a case against me and waited until I was right in position before he struck.

Mood swings, loud negative self-talk, and the boyfriend's soul tie continually pulled me back into the hole I'd once had known intimately. I knew with the help of the Holy Spirit I could make my way out of it, but with Satan's case raging against me, reminding me that I was not out yet, I easily fell back into the hole. He began to use every bit of his arsenal against me: everything in my life that had been hurtful and demeaning. He will, can and does use whatever he can to destroy us. Now I had all these open doors and the oppression beginning to overwhelm and overtake me. DEPRESSION began to come like a flood. Not just some of the time, but all the time. I don't remember when I wasn't depressed. I was in church every time the door opened. Active in all the activities, leading a women's group and I was so depressed I couldn't see my way out. The case was set and the assignment was working, now for the kill.

Depression was now my best friend, something I could depend on and I looked forward to wasting away in it. It was my comfort, my new language, my new friend. Yes, I'd gone to the altar for prayer, I shared with my leaders who prayed, I prayed for myself, but the case was set. Unlike Jesus who fasted and walked in the desert and was tempted by the devil, Jesus had nothing in common with satan. But I did! I had fornication, alcohol, cursing, bad attitude, and negative self-talk. I could go on and on. Open doors to sin were all around me. Hosea 4:6 says "my people are destroyed for lack of knowledge." I didn't know about soul ties, I didn't know that I needed to be delivered from my past sins. I didn't know that I needed to "partner" with the Holy Spirit and follow His lead on how to live my life. No drinks with my dinner, no negative self-talk, and no self-pity. There was a host of things that I had in common with satan and he was using all of it to keep me bound and tied up in depression.

I was just going through the motions because there was no freedom for me. It became my secret, going to church smiling and enjoying my environment in public, but when I got home it was a different story. What you hide in the dark begins to grow and gain life. My depression had grown to thoughts of suicide, which had a loud but soothing voice. Not scary but calming like rubbing a black cat, content and soothing. That was the trick. It wasn't scary but it felt "normal" to meditate on different ways to kill myself. Then I would agree with satan in my self-talk. "Yes, this is the way I could be closer to God." "The word says, to die is gain, right." I began to contemplate how I would do it and what people would say about me after I was gone. This became my way of life, 'light' at church, 'darkness' at home. I'd convinced myself that things would be better. I would show all those who hurt me what it felt like to be hurt; then they would feel guilty about treating me bad. Satan's case was set; I was now having the same thing in common with the devil. That's all he wants, he wants you to see like he sees, feel like he feels and believe like he believes. But it's all a LIE!

Rise Up to Greatness

The first plan was easy; the voice said all I had to do was run my car off the road. Easy enough, I would find myself driving the long way home from church. Highway after highway lulled my body into a numbing state. Not paying attention to the traffic around me just driving and letting the car kind of go anyway it wanted to go. This was easy and mindless. BUT GOD always has a plan!! He set angels to guard around my car so I would not hit anything. The plan of mine NEVER worked! But that did not stop the case against me. I began to isolate in my home not leaving unless I absolutely had to, not doing too much church either. I listened to depressing music and movies to keep feeding the black cat that now lived within me. I reconnected with the "boyfriend" just to get my heart broken again. We all know that once a man has had you, when you call him to have you again, rarely does he say no! The rejection was putting me over the top emotionally. This was the bullet in the gun that satan used to destroy me; the case against me was working. Self-loathing, not eating, voices screaming to do away with myself are now LOUDER! The tears that have become my meat and drink take my body into darker places that I haven't known before. In my distress and despair, I find myself in my bathroom, having a memory of a time where I put a razor to my wrist and the voice was there again, "Go ahead cut yourself, nobody cares if you live or if you die." I realized my soul wasn't all black when a little piece of me cried out to God and said: "Lord you can stop this! If you love me you can make someone call me before I'm finished." And He did, a friend was in my neighborhood and called to see if I was home. She came over immediately and all I could do was cry. Despite the visit, my soul was still black, the abyss continued to call my name and I listened. But the fight in my cried out to God for help; my spirit knew that being with Him was the best place I could be. The fight continued and I began searching the bathroom for anything that I could take to slowly let me slip away. I found some pain pills and began to take them and slowly slipped into a restful place.

    I made it to my bed and went off to sleep. But to my surprise, I woke up. I woke up to the voice of TD Jakes preaching at one of the first Woman Thou Art Loose conferences. He was talking directly to my spirit and my spirit told my soul to wake up. I don't even remember the television being on TBN (Christian television station), a habit I guess. But God always has a plan. That man preached like two worlds on fire and I listened. I heard what he was saying and it was like water washing those pills out of my system. So, I lived another day. I wasn't healed but my soul began to listen. I was able to press into God like I had done so many times before, but this time it was different. There was light coming from inside me that brought peace to my mind. I made it through the day, the week, and the months. Holding on to every morsel of light that came my way, I was still not strong enough to rebound into a rational state of being. The fight took time and a few more confrontations with the 'loud' voice that continued to give me good cause to kill myself. But now the fight continued. The little bit of light was so bright, so healing, so whole. I began to take in more and more of the light until I was able to balance a little better. The color in my world began to come back. Like a black and white movie that was getting a redo, a makeover. As the days unfolded one after the other, I began to apply faith, a little at a time until I was able to get my feelings and emotions together. A life preserver from the Holy Spirit was thrown to me and I held on to it with all my might. Lamentations 3:22-23 says, "It is of the Lord's mercies that we are not consumed because his compassions fail not. They are new every morning: great is thy faithfulness." The word became my lighthouse, my anchor, and my sword of weapon I needed to fight the battle. I began to study this scripture and the entire book of Lamentations. In my studies, the Lord showed me the effects of sin in the world and how to put my hope and trust in Him and not self. I had to take a strong statement of faith, a lighthouse to shine in the midst of the consequences of sin and disobedience. The word of God had everything I needed to make it. What you don't resist means you allow and I was ready for the resistance. I had to begin to live purposefully. Just as I was dying on purpose it was now time to live in purpose. The awakening had begun; the strategies from the Lord were coming in loud and clear. I was able to distinguish the loud demonic, negative voice from the loving peaceful voice of my Savior. It was time to evict the black cat from my home, my mind, and my soul. I literally walked through my apartment declaring the word of the Lord to the evil oppression that had taken residence in my home. I had to be mindful of what was going into my ear gates and eye gates; I had to disconnect the plug. Just as I fed it darkness, now I had to be intentional with putting the light in. This was harder than it sounds because it takes 21 days for a thing to become a habit. The enemy is relying on your laziness to not press in to break bad habits.

But I was at war, the battle was on, my mind was no longer cloudy but clear. Every new day, I had to fight to maintain my FREEDOM I had to CHOOSE life. I chose to disconnect from the spirits that entangled me, like octopus tentacles. The enemy had strategically tied me up like a hostage to depression. I had to cut off/disconnect every soul tie with the enemy one by one. The spirit of oppression, disconnect; the spirit of depression, disconnect; the spirit of self-pity, disconnect! The spirit of pride, death, and suicide – DISCONNECT!!

I had to strategize on how to practice abstinence from sin cycles. What is a sin cycle? Those open doors and the things that give the enemy legal access to your soul! No more alcohol with my meals, no more swear words, no more negative self-talk, and the biggest, no more fornication. I had to choose to live a chaste life and watch how I dressed, how I spoke to men and how I behaved around them. It was a tightening but freeing lifestyle. Only God could bring that kind of peace in the middle of a storm.

Now I was free but had to maintain my light and my glow in Jesus. After repenting, closing doors and taking my life back, it was now my turn to give back. I had to sanctify my heart back to the Father, repent for my pride and for rejecting who and how He made me. I had to release my sins and forgive myself, rebuke and repel all demonic entry ways so I could keep my spirit open to only hear His voice, not the dark loud voice. I began to live a worshipful life of being intimate with the Holy Spirit. His spirit began to fill in the voided spaces of my soul and mind. This freed my heart to serve and serving helped keep me from inverting my emotions, being self-absorbed in my own little world. Not I, but he that "now" lives inside of me. This is how I fought the beasts at Ephesus and won! I chose to fight rather than shrink back in fear. In His strength, I can

Rise Up to Greatness

now live in victory. And, if you have ever found yourself in such a fight, pray this with me.

Let's Pray

Dear Lord Jesus, your love and kindness are better than life, I choose you and I choose life. Revelation 21:5 says "Behold I make all things new and these words are faithful and true." I can now rest in your green pastures because you have dug up my fallow ground and caused me to be fruitful in all areas of my life. I now understand that my body is the temple where the Holy Spirit dwells and I must keep my temple clean. Give me the strength to fight this fight thru to victory. In the name of Jesus, Amen.

Rotten Fruit

"Death and life are in the power of the tongue: and they that love it shall eat the fruit thereof." Proverbs 18:21 (KJV)

When I was a kid, the number one complaint from my teachers during parent/teacher conferences was that I talked too much in class. Great grades, but too much talking! To get in trouble for talking in class, there has to be someone for you to talk to, so there was always someone in one of my classes willing to chat it up and giggle with me. Well, old habits die hard. I am still pretty chatty in certain situations and if there is a person around who is willing to engage, I am ready. However, the people I engage with have changed a bit. I've traded classmates for colleagues and playmates for a soul mate; these are the people who I am most likely to "get caught talking to" these days. Engaging with different types of people about things of a greater substance has shown me a lot about myself over the years. In my adult life, I found that I not only talk a lot, but I'm not always mindful of the potential consequences of what comes out of my mouth.

Enter Shanté, newly wedded wife, who talks a lot and sometimes way too much. I married my husband in 2012 and although things weren't blissful (as they rarely are), they were great. Building a home together was exciting and having a loving person to wake up to every day was nothing short of amazing. Then the honeymoon phase came to a screeching halt. My husband got hurt on his job just three short months after we got married and, in addition to leaving much of the upkeep of our home to me, that made things difficult financially. Adding to the financial difficulty, Super Storm Sandy hit and I was out of work for two weeks. In what seemed like the blink of an eye, my marriage had become something I could've never fathomed it would become. All of these difficulties had a huge effect on my relationship with my husband.

I was frustrated, overwhelmed, and resentful. I was so caught up in my marriage not being what I expected and resenting the turns it had taken, I allocated zero time to be mindful of my words. The typical, and not-so-typical, stresses of marriage created insecurity, frustration, and anger, which I frequently spewed toward my husband. After hearing so much negative, my husband shut down, which made me spew negative things even more. In my mind, what I had to say was important and was supposed to affect positive change in my household, even if the content and delivery were absolutely terrible. My words were like darts and my sentiments were like spears. I had allowed my overwhelming emotions to make a weapon of mass destruction out of my tongue and my marriage was the entity being destroyed.

About three and half years into my marriage, I realized that things had just about fallen apart. There was an emotional wedge between us my mouth created. I felt extremely guilty, helpless, and hopeless all at the same time. I felt defeated and often asked God why things had gotten so terrible and why He hadn't fixed it sooner. After quite some time of having a "personal pity party" God gently showed me that many of the trials we experienced as a couple I'd literally spoken into existence. During many of my mindless rants, I spoke negative things concerning my husband and marriage. I spewed words that I could not take back and that were slowly pushing us further apart. That was a difficult pill to swallow and all the emotions I spewed at my husband for those years paled in comparison to the guilt I felt.

We've now been married for just over four years, and I've accepted that in order for a shift to truly happen, it has to start with me. Even though I experience some of the same emotions from time to time, I am ever so mindful of my words, and make daily efforts to build my home with my words instead of tearing it down. It's a process for someone who has lived a life of saying what she wants when she wants with little thought about how it affects others or outcomes, but a process worth hanging in there for. If God had not given me that reminder, I believe that instead of being on life support, my marriage would be dead right now. So I am thankful for God's humbling revelation and the strength to apply it to my life because my faith tells me that my marriage will be better for it.

Let's Pray
Father God, thank you for your still small voice. Thank you for using your creations to reveal your heart for us and for being a mirror in which we see our truest selves. I ask that you show us the parts of ourselves that are not like you so that we might become mindful not to let them abort the destiny that you have for us. Help us to season our words with salt and to always speak in love, even when we are hurting. Please allow us to let our lights shine through our actions and our words, so that you may get the glory out of the positive things that result. Remind us to speak those things that are of you, about you, and glorifying to you. In Jesus' name, Amen.

His Joy

On a beautiful fall morning, I sat with a friend on her patio next to a canal behind her home. It was quiet and just beautiful. We have been friends for 20 plus years but we had not seen each other for several months and were taking the time to catch up. In the midst of our conversation, I was asked if I remembered what John 10:10 had to say. I said, "I have come that you might have life and have it to the full." My friend said, " Yes, but do you remember the first part?" 'The thief comes to steal, kill and destroy.' I was sharing with her all that had transpired in my life over that past year. How the thief tried to come between me and what God had planned for my life; to destroy my joy in the season I was in and to steal all the life out of it. I most assuredly didn't want that, I believe no one would. My friend went on to say, "just tell that thief and liar, no!" Because satan does come to kill, steal and destroy but God has come that we might have life and have it to the fullest.

Throughout my life, I have been told many things and not so many nice things. Not much that was uplifting, very little that would build me up, pretty much nothing that would make me think I had any value whatsoever and not much that made me want to strive to be, anything in life.

I believed those lies from people I should have been able to trust, it took me years and godly kind people to get me out of that mindset. If you have experienced these lies, it is not who you are. One of the most important things in life you need to know is who you are in Christ. Your identity is found in Him not in what others say about you or what wrong choices you made in your past. Do those choices change who you become? Yes! But your identity is always found in Him.

Whatever you may be dealing with in your life right now, know that in everything there is life. In your right now you can choose joy. Satan does want to steal your life. He wants to kill your joy and to lie to you that your life is hopeless and he is the one telling you, you

Rise Up to Greatness

can't do it. God's grace is sufficient and His power is perfect in your weakness. In everything, we can give thanks. Don't ever forget the One who loves you and endured it all, for you. Remember:

- You are a woman who was made in God's perfect image and He loves you.
- You are a woman who finds her worth in God and not what others think or say about you.
- You are a woman who is accepted by God.
- You are a woman whose uniqueness is needed and you have His grace.
- You are a woman who is not perfect but you have God's mercy.

You are a woman! A woman when seeking God's heart daily will know that the lies she has heard throughout her life aren't true. Especially the ones in her head! Listen, we all have difficulties and challenges in our lives sometimes. We make mistakes, we live, and we learn, we are human, we are not perfect and that is ok. Put your faith in Him, trust and know that you are created for a purpose and are loved by God. Jesus wants to take the joy that He has and place it in you. Choose joy. It's not always easy but God does not want you to stay in the stress and the difficult times, He wants happiness for us. His Joy!

- Joy in caring for loved ones.
- Joy is being there for each other in the hard times.
- Joy is in serving others.
- Joy is in persevering, pushing thru those tough times.
- Joy is in becoming what God wants you to be.
- Joy is in what is to come and joy is in loving like He does.

You can choose joy, even on the tough days. Rest in Him knowing that joy is ok and that joy is what He wants for you. He said, 'Never will I leave you. Never will I forsake you.' He promised. I truly believe this for your life. Let the joy of the Lord be bigger than the lies in your head and the lies you were told. Only believe His truth. Every story is unique and each story, including yours, is important to God. Brokenness does not have to be the final chapter, it just doesn't. Begin to imagine what you look like in the hands of God...oh my! This opens the door to hope. Jesus is not afraid of our brokenness, hold out your hands and open those doors, move those walls that are so carefully guarding your pain and let God carry all of it for you. It's not too late to become all that you are created to be. Every time you push through those hard times and choose joy you are making a way to your dreams and pushing all those lies out of you. Turn all those lies over to God and allow Him to heal all those broken pieces, it may take a little time but always be ready for your healing, be equipped by reading His word daily and by all means know that your destiny is in His hands.

"I have told you this so that my Joy may be in you and that your joy may be complete." John 15:11

Let's Pray
Father God we belong to you. I pray for the women who read this that they start seeing your life with them as a relationship and find in their most difficult times a miraculous joy that can only be received from you. I pray that their relationship with you grows strong and deep Father. I ask that you heal each and every reader from their brokenness and that they begin to know your love, grace, and mercy in their lives. Help them, Father, to choose happiness and thank you for your joy for I know it is what you want for all of us. In your precious name, Amen.

Christ is The Invisible Image

I remember many years ago a very dear friend of mine asked me a simple question; "what made you so excited about God?" She knew me very well for she is one of my best friends. We went to high school together, and she went through one of my most painful struggles with me. So when she asked, I knew she wanted to understand why did Selina, the girl that had a knack for manipulating, getting her way, not always being kind, all of a sudden find God? The truth is I don't think at the time I answered her question wholeheartedly because I was still trying to figure that out myself. What I know is that I was a broken young woman.

Think about it, I was around 20 and married with two kids. There was a weight on my shoulders over something I had done as a teenager, and I had no idea how to be a mom or a wife. I was determined to make it happen one way or another. However, I fell to pieces. But God!
Today, I want to answer that question now, to my dear friend who we will call Violet. I have always believed there was a God; I grew up knowing that. However, He was presented to me as someone to fear at all times; not the loving and forgiving God I know Him to be now. What got me excited about Christ was that I felt lost, confused, hurt, and without hope and giving my heart to Him renewed my life. The hurt would take time to heal but I knew there was healing coming. There was so much on my shoulders, so much guilt pain and then the responsibility of taking care of a family. It was so much to deal with. The biggest burden was not knowing who I was and feeling so utterly and totally rejected. The one thing that I remembered the most and will forever stay in my heart is the week my husband committed his life to the Lord. We visited church all week and every time we went someone would approach me and say without fail, "God loves you!" "God truly loves you," "Do you know how much God loves you?" Honestly, at first, it was like nails on a chalkboard but little did I know it was what I needed to hear. Those people were

making the invisible God a visible image to me by showing me love. Authentic love!

It's hard to accept love from a stranger, but there is something about a person who has completely devoted their lives to Christ, there is something so unique, so different you can't shake it. The truth is you are either drawn to them, or you run the other way because you cannot take what they are giving. I was taken from a place of such brokenness and felt like new; like everything I was ever told about love and who I was meant nothing until that very moment. I encountered restored hope and joy in ways I never thought was possible. Much of what I am writing is hard to express because until you can capture it in your own heart, it can never be fully understood. All I know is that I found a part of me I did not know was lost. All I wanted to do was share it with everyone I knew and would meet. Don't get me wrong; life isn't perfect because my life has changed. However, every trial I have dealt with in the years to follow were met with a different type of response.

Have you ever in your life felt hopeless? During the times I did, I never fully understood it. Where could I go? Who could I turn too? I had a love of family and friends but what I was dealing with what no one could fix. It was Christ the visible image of the invisible God that changed my life. He came through a friend, a stranger, a butterfly, my children and my spouse. Christ wanted to reveal himself in the same ways to you. Will you allow Him to step in? Will you allow your heart to see the invisible God through every person you meet? The verse is found in Colossians 1:15 "Christ is the visible image of the invisible God. He existed before anything that was created and is supreme over all creation,"

He was here before anything was created and He knew everything I would need or want or even desire. He was aware that I would need to see His love expressed to me through others and that in receiving His love, in that way, would allow me to do the same for everyone I met.

Let's Pray

Father, I ask that as we pray, you begin to show yourself in tangible ways to my sister who is reading this. It is my desire that you be ever present over her life. Throughout her day and week from the time she wakes that she sees you in everything. Even in the moments that are hard and lonely, she will feel you are there. I pray a new hope be deeply rooted within her spirit. I pray her heart be healed of pain or misrepresented love. I ask that you will immerse her entirely in your love and that even as we pray now that you begin to send others that will stand with her and walk with her during her time of need. I pray against all doubt about who you are and that she would feel the joy and love of who you are in her life at all times. I pray that in the silence of night that she senses the music of heaven being serenaded over her as she rests. I ask these things in Jesus name, Amen.

Letting Go

My words fly up
My prayers hit the wall
No answer I get
No answer at all.
I'm confused and stagnant
Not growing the least
Answer me, Father
Answer me, please.
I've had enough
Of trying alone
I've had enough
Of taking control.
It's not my place
To pretend I'm You.
I'm not even close
To being worthy of You.
Struggles and Problems
Weighing me down
I want to Let Go
But I don't know How.
Teach me, please
To be dependent on You
Teach me, please
To Let Go
I'm through

I must confess there have been many times in my life where I hit the bottom of the barrel. I tried to do life on my own and pushed Jesus to the back burner while saying, "I got this Lord". Or instead of running to Jesus with my worries or pain, I would band aid the issue or suppress it. The result was like a snowball effect where after I try life on my own, I then become stagnant in my walk. My

Rise Up to Greatness

problems and worries build and then I find myself complaining to the Lord about it. Oh, my audacity is shameful and I often wondered how God could use me when I act in such a manner. However, in moments like this, the Holy Spirit often reminds me of King David in the Bible. He was considered "a man after God's own heart" and yet even he took matters into his own hands and had dry spells with the Lord. In 2 Samuel 11, we can read about David, Bathsheba and the sin committed. Instead of taking his sin and problems to the Lord, David tried to cover it up and do it all on his own. Of course, as with David, our sin and need for control distances us from the Lord. We then question, "God where are you? Why can't I hear you?" In Psalms 13:1 ESV David cries out, "How long, O Lord? Will you forget me forever? How long will you hide your face from me?" Even recently, there have been times where I've asked the Lord, "Are you even listening to me anymore, I can't hear you or feel you. Lord, I feel like I'm talking to the wall." Don't get me wrong; sometimes our feeling of stagnancy and distance from the Lord is not necessarily in part to a sin, but to our own complacency or apathy in pursuing Him and His presence. I find that many times I let my feelings and emotions control my actions and thoughts, as if I have to feel the Lords' presence or experience a certain emotion to know that He is there. Then if I don't have such an experience, I start to pull back in seeking Him and here comes the snowball effect I spoke of previously. One of my biggest struggles is that I constantly have to remind myself that I'm not in control, it's not all about feelings or emotions and that I need to seek the Lord daily, not just because I feel like it, but because He is worthy!

If we are honest with ourselves, many of us have felt this way at one point or another. So how do we break the vicious cycle? The first step is admitting that *we* can't do anything, "for apart from [Jesus] you can do nothing."—John 15:5 ESV.
We must assume responsibility for our actions or lack thereof and confess that we need His divine intervention in our lives. Second, ask the Lord to reveal any seeds or roots that may lie deep within. This will not be an easy process. Honesty and vulnerability with yourself and the Lord are a must. Last, make it a habit of taking your struggles, worries, and desires to the foot of the cross daily.

Rise Up to Greatness

In confessing and seeking the Lord daily, chains will start to break and the enemy's hold on you will lessen. It will be a battle and the enemy won't go without a fight, so stay in the Word and prayed up. It's also beneficial to not walk this path alone, if you have a spiritual mentor or close friend in the Lord, ask them to pray with you, pour into you and to help keep you accountable. Keep in mind this will be a process and not a quick overnight change. Please don't discount yourself for the Lord's work just because you have struggles or issues. Remember King David and how the Lord used him mightily even though he had a rap sheet.

Here are some verses to meditate on:

"Behold, I am with you always, to the end of the age" Matthew 28:20 (ESV)

"If then you have been raised with Christ, seek the things that are above, where Christ is, seated at the right hand of God. *Set your minds on things that are above, not on things that are on earth." Colossians 3:1-2 (ESV)*

"You will seek me and find me when you seek me with all your heart." Jeremiah 29:13 (ESV)

"The righteous cry and the Lord hears, and delivers them out of all their troubles." Psalm 34:17. (NASB)

"This is the confidence that we have in Him that if we ask anything according to His will, He hears us." 1 John 5: 14 (ESV)

"My flesh and my heart may fail, but God is the strength of my heart and my portion forever." Psalm 73:26 (ESV)

<u>Let's Pray</u>
Heavenly Father I thank you that no matter what we have done, You still love us and are waiting with arms wide open for us to come running back to You. I pray for Your strength over my dear sister.

Strength that she would call on you in times of trouble, strength to confess the issues that are weighing her down, and strength to keep on going even when it all feels overwhelming. I pray for divine interventions in her life where she can't deny Your presence and Your love for her. I ask Lord for Godly influences to infiltrate her life and those she needs to let go of to be removed. I thank you, Lord, that it is not about feelings and emotions and that Your love remains constant no matter what we feel. Thank you, Father, for the plans You have for her and I ask for your guidance and protection over her life. I ask all these things in Jesus name, Amen!

Beware Of The Weeds

Matthew 13:38 "The field is the world, and the good seed stands for the people of the kingdom. The weeds are the people of the evil one." (NIV)

Instead of using the leadership gift that God gave me in my career, I had to go the long way around. When God has gifted you with all His spiritual gifts, there's always one or two that tend to stand out a little more than others. The problem is sometimes we are not aware of what the special ones are right away. Have you ever had someone say, "Oh you're so good at this or you're so good at that?" Take the hint; He's trying to let you know that you're to shine a little brighter in that area. The spotlight of His anointing on you is also seen by satan. He is also seeking whom he can kill and destroy. John 10:10 (NIV) says "the thief comes only to steal and kill and destroy." And, he knows when you are shining with the anointing of God.
I had a friend tell me once that the devil only messes with those who are a threat to his kingdom. He doesn't waste his time on those who are his and are not advancing the kingdom of God, and I believe this. Satan is adamant and relentless with his pursuits against us and he will stop at nothing to destroy what God has created. His favorite weapon to use against us is the human being. We tend to fall into his trap so easily, he uses your family, friends, employers and even strangers. Unfortunately, we are easily swayed when it comes to his demonic opportunities.

I once had a job where I was an administrator for two bosses. They were as opposite as night and day. One was from the North and the other was from the South. They had totally different styles and the way they did things. I could go on and on about their differences, but the biggest difference was one recognized my shining spotlight and the other didn't. She discerned my potential, my character, and integrity. The other saw none of the above and it made her cringe every time she saw me. The only thing we all had in common is that

Rise Up to Greatness

we all "said" we believed in God and that we were Christians. But I believe one of them had given herself over to the devil because she had dark ways about her. Now that I am older I realized that her negative response was a response to the Spirit of God alive in me. In 2 Corinthians 6:15 "Can people who follow the Lord have anything in common with those who don't?" (CEV)

We worked in a small office, in tight quarters, and that became a real challenge. It was hard to have private conversations or meetings without one hearing what the other was saying. This became the perfect set up for the enemy to use the flesh to aggravate the situation. 1 John 1: 5-7 says that "God is light, and in Him is no darkness at all. If we say we have fellowship with Him and yet walk in darkness, we lie and do not practice the truth; but if we walk in the light, as He Himself is in the light, we have fellowship with one another, and the blood of Jesus His Son cleanses us from all sin."(NASB)
If we say we believe in the love of Christ Jesus, why would this situation be such a problem? Because one of us had given self over to satan, he began to whisper things in her ear. Once she began to believe the lies, she acted out against me.

I could feel the atmosphere beginning to shift, and the war was on. She first complained about my work, nitpicking everything I did. I had to comply because she was my boss. Then she complained that I was way too friendly and I needed to focus more on what I was doing for "her" and not the other boss. She began to manifest with a "tit for tat" score sheet in the office. After a while, there was no pleasing her no matter what I did. The behavior went on for a while until the other boss realized I was starting to change. My light was not as bright, something was wrong, but she couldn't put her finger on it. I wasn't going to tell her what was happening to me because I wasn't quite sure myself. It was a setup, the spirit of intimidation always finds a crack in the door, and it won't stop until it has broken the door down. The signs to look for when this spirit comes knocking is second guessing yourself. Feeling like you're missing something during conversations so you "over listen". Those feelings add to the second guessing of your thoughts. Your self-confidence begins to melt; I say melt because it starts slowly fading before you realize you've missed your "sound mind." At the end of every day, I felt I left a little bit more of me on the floor of that office. I began to second guess myself, make silly mistakes, and not smile much. I began to turn inward, the siege on my light made my spirit look like a piece of paper with holes in it.

I don't remember how long this went on before the next wave of the storm began to hit my mind and emotions. The storm began to turn into a tornado. It started one evening when she asked me to stay late to help her with something. I agreed, thinking nothing of it. I busied myself at my desk and noticed out of the corner of my eye that she locked the main office door after the last person left. You know how you think in your subconscious that, hmm that was odd. However, your brain just keeps going like nothing's wrong? Well, that's what I did; I just kept going. She walked back to her office and asked me to bring a project that we were working on, so I complied. I sat in the chair in front of her desk and again, she gets up and closes the door to her office. Now I'm like, this "IS" odd, but brain still not sure what to think. She takes my copy of the project and begins to tear it apart and tear me apart along with it. This goes on and on until now she is screaming at me, at the top of her lungs, so loud, so long! I was taken by surprise and never even tried to defend my work or what she was saying to me, it was all so surreal. But the door was already down, satan had been working on me for weeks, my defenses were down, I had no fight. She finally finished and dismissed me like a dog that peed on the floor. BAM!! My door was just broken down by the spirit of intimidation; the persecution had begun.

Week after week, we would have these little "pow wows". She would tear into me, up one side and down the other. If it wasn't my work, it was my clothes and even complained that I wasn't "Black" enough and wasn't living up to what she called a regular Black person. What? Are you kidding me!! Satan had gone down into my guts to destroy me! He is ruthless and will stop at nothing to derail you and your sense of worth. If you let him, he will even challenge your identity, he will undo everything that you think you know. And when your defenses are down, you will open yourself to any assault without even putting up a fight. Attacking my "Blackness" was her favorite, each week she came up with a new way to teach me about Black people. Did she not see that I was already a Black woman? She did every stereotypical thing to show me that I was doing the Black thing all wrong, according to what she believed. Really? Maybe she was doing the Black thing all wrong! Maybe she was doing the Christian thing all wrong! Maybe she was doing the human being thing ALL WRONG! That spirit had me so trained that if I didn't say or do exactly what she wanted there would be another meeting or beating of the mouth after work. She pulled out all the stops: locked doors; screaming and yelling; intimidation, and hatred. The behavior began to escalate and once she called me into her office, screaming and yelling at me and banging on her desk with her fists. Every hit, I would envision my face or body being punched under the weight of her heavy, big hands. I was so afraid and mad at myself for allowing this woman to immobilize me, to turn me into a frightened little girl. I could not tell anyone or do anything and was now the hostage of this demonic attack.

Have you ever heard of the spirit of python? I was right in the belly of this spiritual beast. The Python spirit is a form of divination. The characteristics are just like the snake; it constricts and slowly squeezes its prey to death. This spirit wraps itself around its victim, which can be a person, family, church, or office, and he slowly squeezes the life out of them. This spirit shows up in Acts 16:16 against Paul in Macedonia and it is still working today. I was a victim of this spiritual squeezing and choking of my words, my joy, and my spirit. The manifestations of this spirit are weariness, confusion, discouragement, and frustration. I had all the symptoms of being snake food. I wanted to leave this job but I felt so helpless; the pressure, heaviness, and depression, were unbearable. I was tight in its grip.

My other boss would ask me if things were okay, she was noticing little changes in me. And of course, I would say, "yes everything is fine". What a lie! Isn't it just like that bullying spirit that would make you lie to cover up your attacker. Why is that? But I did, week after week until she finally took me out of the office to lunch and I just broke down. Crying and spilling my guts, but I was still trapped, still a hostage. Isn't it funny when you are trapped with fear, that praying becomes the last thing that you do? Prayer should have been the first thing I did to end the destruction against me. But oh no, like so many of us, we just let satan sucker punch us over and over again until we finally drag our limp, bruised carcass to the edge of the boxing ring and tag Jesus in to take it from there. THANK YOU, JESUS! You were just waiting for me to get to the end of myself, to call on your great name to rescue me. I began to pray in the name of Jesus to break the power of that snake off me, to give me holy boldness to get the job done. I used the word, the blood of Jesus and, the most powerful of all, the authority of Jesus Christ to break and destroy that deadly spirit. I prayed for courage because I had allowed fear to take up residency in my mind. The fear of man was manipulating me into believing I was less than who God made me. I also felt like the grace for my boss was getting ready to run out. Isaiah 59:19 (NKJV) says "when the enemy comes in like a flood, the Spirit of the Lord will lift up a standard against him." I've always interpreted this scripture to mean, when satan has done the best he can do, given his best punch, THEN the Spirit of the Lord will come in and wipe him out!! But it is actually God's promise that He is there as soon as the enemy comes against us!

My hero Jesus rescued me from that job. We had a client who would visit us often and comment on how impressed he was with my work. He'd always say, "I would love to have you come and work for our company." We all took it as a joke each time he said it. But one day I asked him in private if he was serious and he said yes, if I ever wanted to make a career change, he would hire me in a minute. And he did. But that's not all; I must give credit to the enemy for being a relentless foe. That mean, hateful, child of God boss of mine tried not to pay me my last paycheck and my 2 weeks of vacation pay. I had to go to the Department of Labor and file a formal complaint against her. And you don't have to ask, yes, she did have to pay me all of it, every penny of it! The snake doesn't let you go easily, you have to fight, fight with all your might. And when it finally lets you go. KILL IT! I mean machete knife kill it! Go into your prayer closet and wear him out! Reclaim your spirit, your mind, and your strength. Use the holy boldness that God gives us and as they say, storm hell with a water gun and go get yourself back. Don't allow wickedness in high places to hover over your head. Be spiritually alert, pay attention to your surroundings. When the Holy Spirit gives you that check in your spirit, don't dismiss it, or second-guess it. This is your lifeline to Life. In John 7:38 (KJV) it says, "He that believeth on me, as the scripture hath said out of his belly shall flow rivers of living water." Be sensitive to the Holy Spirit, pay attention, keep your head up and trust your gut, because your gut doesn't lie.

Let's Pray
Pray this periodically in your quiet times: Spirit of the Living God, I submit to the power and authority you have over my life. I thank you that your promises for me are yes and amen, and you do all things well. I believe you are the doorkeeper to my heart and mind. Nothing is too hard for you. You are my healer and the lifter of my head. Your resurrection power transcends through the ages and counteracts all the works of the evil one. Now, by the Authority of Jesus Christ, I come against every power of darkness, witchcraft, hexes, curses, and incantations that have been spoken over me. I apply the powerful blood of Jesus over my life, keeping me from all hurt, harm, and danger. In the mighty name of Jesus, Amen.

Family

"Family is the most important thing in the world."
–Princess Diana

Reclaimed My Marriage

God's divine intervention was most obvious when in my most pathetic state. I'll explain!

I grew up in an Italian household. I was the only female with 3 brothers. My parents were from Italy and we were first generation Americans. All my life I was expected to learn to cook, keep a clean house and get married. My brothers, on the other hand, had the word 'college' buzzing around their heads, but not me. I was an average student in high school, didn't do my best because of the crowd. It wasn't my drive that didn't make me excel; I had no goals. I did, however, by the grace of God, enroll myself into a Medical Assistant training school because the medical field was interesting to me. I always used to say I wanted to be a pediatrician. Did I get encouraged to do so? No, not really. It was too much money and I wouldn't have the grades to accomplish that dream.

I finished the Medical Assistant Program and got a job in a medical office. I was getting closer to my goal of being a pediatrician! Not really working and enjoying my job, I also became a fitness instructor, working with youth and closer to my goal as a pediatrician!

Something happened to my parents! My father was a tractor trailer driver and found a tract about salvation through Jesus on his windshield. And, THEY GOT SAVED! My siblings and I were like, what the heck, no more Catholic church? My parents, especially my rule with an Iron Fist father, were kinder and gentler. So naturally, we all took advantage of that! But, my parents were praying us all in.

I started going to church with my then biker boyfriend. We would go to church and then go out to the bars right after church. At the time, I didn't know that my future husband, Paul, had noticed that I was attending. Well, since I had a mob of people praying for me, those visits became more frequent and more uncomfortable.

The Holy Spirit was tugging at my heart. I had to break it off with my boyfriend; he wasn't into the church scene.

Paul was on the scene quicker than I anticipated! He actually told his brother he was going to marry me as I was just visiting the church with my then boyfriend! He claimed me! Well, we got married, had three daughters within six years. We were doing it, the whole married life, going to church, etc. Life was good!

At about year 12 into the marriage, things started to unravel. I was complaining that I got married too young; (at 20) I never had my freedom and I started to go out with girlfriends and played the single life. I was all over the place looking for excitement, fulfillment. Even though I thought I was still serving God, I wasn't. It was a lie! I didn't have God's Word written on my heart and ill-equipped to avoid temptation, which seized me. My focus was shifted to selfish desires. But thank God there was a way out, I just didn't grab at it right away. I got so entangled with the world I was unfaithful to my husband.

Paul was at home holding down the fort with our 3 young children and received advice from multiple people to get rid of me. Surely he had grounds for it, but he kept praying. I thank God for my praying husband. We lived together but had separate lives. When I reflect back, how the heck was I doing this? Right under his nose! What a mess I was and I listened to all the lies like, I got married too young, I missed all the fun, now I am stuck.

We were fighting all the time. At this time domestic abuse was on everyone's radar, especially after the OJ Simpson trial. One night we were fighting and I threatened to call the police, so I did. They asked me if I was afraid, I said yes, like a fool. So they handcuffed my husband and took him to jail. The worst thing possible, but also the best thing, I'll explain.

The next day we went to court, the District Attorney was a Christian. She said you have two choices, serve time or go to Marriage Counseling! She recommended Marriage Ministries and we never saw her again. To this day, I am convinced she was an angel. "Do not forget to show hospitality to strangers, for by so doing some people have shown hospitality to angels without knowing it."—Hebrews 13:2 Of course, we went the counseling route which was 13 weeks. We had the best mentors that we still speak with today, but back then, I went kicking and screaming up until week 3. Although I had to go to counseling, I was still going out with friends!

One night I came home and completely surrendered and saw how pathetic my life was. My husband had had enough but was still willing to love me and in a quick moment, I saw his eyes change into Jesus's eyes. I will say that again! I saw his eyes change into Jesus's eyes and HE was looking at me. JESUS WAS LOOKING AT ME!!! The look of LOVE that I felt was overwhelming! I was weeping; I dropped to my knees in front of my husband a broken person ready for a healing. "All that the Father gives me will come to me, and whoever comes to me I will never cast out"—John 6:37. You see, God never left me, I left Him. I never pushed Him out of my life. I just wanted it both ways.

Now our marriage is the best ever! We continue to do things to strengthen it. We are blessed to not only love but like each other! We have triumphed and overcame by the grace of God. Something that could've split us was turned around through prayer and commitment.

Let's Pray
Say this prayer when you feel like the grass is greener on the other side:
Lord, please help me to see what I have. Help me to not compare myself to anyone. I am uniquely made and I am perfect in your sight. I do not have to seek others approval, I have yours. I am worthy of this because I am your child.

One Nation Under God

Psalms 133:1 "How good and pleasant it is when God's people live together in peace!" (NIRV)

Sometimes life throws us a curve ball, we think or believe one thing and it turns out to be something else. We're full of hope and promise to believe that all of God's children should get along, could and should love one another. But it's a known fact that the most segregated time in America is 11:00 a.m. Sunday morning. Some of us try really hard to undo this statistic and others are just content with who and where they are. Of course, this is not always how it should be, but it is.

Growing up my parents raised us to love EVERYBODY, no matter their status in life or the color of their skin. It was just one of the rules of our home, things you teach your children as you mold their minds for adulthood. We were taught that God made all the little children, red and yellow, black and white, all are precious in His sight. Unfortunately, I have been challenged with keeping my heart open to what I was taught to believe because the enemy will always test the good in you with evil. We HAVE to choose good, we HAVE to walk in love and see people through the eyes of Christ. We must put on our Jesus glasses.

Have you ever had to church shop? When you move to a new city or a new neighborhood and need to find a new church home. You're looking for something specific, a special place, a church that you "think" is safe, full of love and feels like home with warm anointed fuzzies. Where you could eventually be able to call this 'body' of believers your church family. So, what do you call a church that practices the exact opposite of these virtues that you're looking for, surely not the house of God, surely not your church family?

My family moved to a small rural like community. We church shopped for a while before we settled on this one church. The good singing and the loving pastors I believe is what really won us over.

They were from up north but had been in the south for a while. We really liked their style, teaching, and genuine nature and could see ourselves calling them our "church family". We attended for a while before we decided to plug into some of the activities and outreaches they had available and weren't really concerned that there were not any people attending that looked like us. It was just not an issue for us, but it was for them, so we soon found out. We believed what the Bible said in John 13:34 (NKJV) when Jesus told his disciples before he ascended into heaven, "to love one another." I guess not everyone read and believed that part of the scripture. We did the best we could to blend in with the activities, Bible studies and prayer meetings. It appeared on the surface that we were making headway into becoming a part of our new church family, that all was well. But there was an undercurrent brewing in this place that we were not aware of.

One Sunday after service the pastors asked us if we would like to join their family for a birthday celebration for their grandson. What a special invitation to be included in this family event, of course, we said yes. The upcoming Saturday was the big day, we were so excited, how nice of them to include us. We arrived at the house to find that it was overflowing with people from the church; the church singers, leaders and their families and a few other families as well. It was good to see them and this would give us a needed opportunity to get to know our "church family" better. It was nice to hear them mingling in the kitchen preparing food, the hustle, and bustle setting things up like a real family. We gathered our things and put them in the living room and headed toward the back of the house. We still hadn't seen the pastors yet, we later found out they were in the backyard with all the little ones, playing games and enjoying themselves. We followed the roar of the celebration in the kitchen, with smiles on our faces and excitement in our heart, eager to be a part of the celebration. As we headed in that direction to our shock and amazement as soon as we hit the corner of the kitchen, all the celebration ceased! All eyes turned to us and they weren't friendly eyes, I even heard someone that was sitting at the table mumble "what are they doing here." The person that was standing in front of them at the table nudged them quickly, but it was too late. We heard and saw more than we wanted too. You could imagine our faces, they fell like a ton of bricks, and we were so disappointed. We quickly ushered our daughter through the back door to join the other children that were playing in the backyard. We didn't want to subject her to those evil spirits that shot their ugly, hateful darts into our spirits any longer. It took us both a moment to recover because after we got back in the house the coldness of the room was still lingering. We found ourselves staying outside with the children the rest of the party time; it was the friendliest place to be. It was a long day for us.

We wrestled with what the next plan of action would be. We were still the new kids on the block and we chose them to be our "church family". This was painful. Did we not see this coming, what did we miss? We decided to keep silent for a little while, to pray over how to respond to such behavior. We needed to be sensitive to what the Holy Spirit wanted to do and didn't want to bring more wounds to this wounded group of people. We needed divine intervention. God really manifested himself in a unique way, because when we came back to church and sat among the congregation, they began to display who they were and decided not to interact with us. The people we sat next to turned their bodies away from us on the pews, with their backs toward us, their body language was speaking loud and clear. When pastor said to turn to your neighbor and say such and such, they turned every way, but toward us, as if we were not there, invisible. This was the telltale sign from God that we were marked to make a change in this "church family." This was not the first church we'd become a part of that had treated us less than what God's plan for his people should be.

We decided to share our experience with the pastors. They were so compassionate with their response to us, they wanted to fix it right away by calling them out and confronting each one of them. We said, "No, we don't want you to call them out like that. They would feel like they were being called to the principal's office and would be defensive. Maybe you could handle it from the pulpit with a sermon on love or something." Their hearts were truly wounded by what hurt us, this was what family does, they were genuine. We felt peace that it was brought to light and prayerfully the light of the love of Christ could take over and correct their hearts. We looked forward to pastor's sermon and wanted to stay with our new church family. But it did not go the way we thought it would. At the Wednesday night service, we showed up like nothing was wrong. A few of the leaders that were at the party were there. We were cordial and enjoyed the service. I excused myself to go to the restroom, which was near the pastor's office. His wife had called me into the office to hug my neck about the situation. She then insisted calling a few of the ladies in to sit down and discuss what happened. I refused profusely, but it was too late, one of the ladies was also on her way to the restroom. She called her into the office told her to go get the other one and the four of us had it out. It was not pretty; I was right, they were defensive because they were caught off guard. We dialogued the entire night's service, with no resolve. One of the ladies tried to work it out by saying, "some of my best friends are...", which means I'm open to other people, I just don't know how to do it. It also means that maybe something in her past challenged her love for all of God's people. But with the right interaction, she could possibly change. On the other hand, the other lady, unfortunately, was very bitter and very angry. She even began to scream that she would NEVER EVER be nice to people like us that come to her church! It was her church and she did not want these kinds of people coming!

      The dialogue transpired from bad to worse, it was awful. Regrettably, this woman was obviously not raised to love all of God's children. I believe this is a learned behavior that the enemy uses to keep the spirit of division going. Matthew 12:34(NIV) says "for the mouth speaks what the heart is full of and a good man brings good things out of the good stored up in him, and an evil man brings evil things out of the evil stored up in him."

Ok, let's talk, what's really going on here? This was clearly a hot button for her, an open wound that probably started when she was a young girl. She had not let the chief physician do surgery on her heart. This process cannot be avoided. He needs to cut open the wound, clean it out and allow the Balm of Gilead to heal her wounded heart and make her whole. Anything that is not taken care of at the cross will always be that sore in your soul. When bumped, the scab will fall off and you potentially will discharge your sickness on everyone in your path. The enemy uses the spirit of division and unforgiveness to keep fueling hatred and anger. Only Jesus can cut out what does not belong inside of you, give you a new heart and mind to love his creation, you must submit to the process! A. W. Tozer says it so beautifully, "the reason why so many are still troubled, still seeking, still making little forward progress is because they haven't yet come to the end of themselves. We're still trying to give orders, and interfering with God's work within us." Take note, when you do not allow God to mentor your children (Isaiah 54:13 NIV) you are setting them up to fail. You will leave their spirits open to whatever evil is out there. We need the strategies of heaven to raise our children, secure our marriages and help us live a prosperous life.

Our situation at this church, unfortunately, went from bad to worse. We found out that one of the women's family had been in this church since the beginning and they felt they had a right to decide who comes and who goes, despite what the pastors wanted for their congregation. This disease of discrimination began to fester like cancer. We had uncovered this spirit and it wasn't happy. No matter how much we walked in love and compassion, it just kept growing. They needed more than what we were doing and they were not open to any change. Regrettably, we ended up leaving this body of believers. It took us awhile to recover and to find another congregation; we had to start all over again.

Let's self-reflect, are you any of the people in this story? It does not have to be racism that fuels your hatred and anger. It could be any number of hurts or issues in your life that causes disunity in the Body of Christ. Check yourself, allow the Holy Spirit to get under your feelings and do surgery on your heart. Don't walk in deception, sitting in the house of God like cancer, being the problem and not the solution. God has to work in you before He can work through you. We must all be a vessel that He can flow through. The Message Bible says it best, Romans 12:1-2 "So here's what I want you to do, God helping you: Take your everyday, ordinary life of sleeping, eating, going-to-work and walking around and place it before God as an offering. Embracing what God does for you is the best thing you can do for him. Don't become so well-adjusted to your culture that you fit into it without even thinking. Instead, fix your attention on God. You'll be changed from the inside out. Readily recognize what he wants from you, and quickly respond to it. Unlike the culture around you, always dragging you down to its level of immaturity, God brings the best out of you, develops well-formed maturity in you."

The word of God says in Job 22:28 KJV, "we can decree and declare a thing and it shall be established and the light shall shine upon our ways." So, if there is any area of your life that is still bound up, I decree and declare over you the spirit of freedom and liberty that sets the captive free. Why? Because we are all one nation under God.

Let's Pray
Father God, your ways are higher than our ways, so teach us, mold us, renew a right spirit in us, that we may be used to uplift and build your kingdom here on earth. Help us to dig deep, roots of love, so like a tree planted by the rivers of living water, our branches will be strong and full of the fruits of the spirit to reach a sin sick world. Heal the broken places within us and use our pain as a vehicle to bridge the gap of division in our church family where the enemy has broken the bond of unity. In the name of Jesus, Amen.

The Fight for Community

For as long as I can remember, I always dreamt of moving into my own apartment in a fast-paced city, all alone, and not knowing anyone. Even as a young girl, this desire was slightly peculiar, due to the fact that I loved being around friends and family and had no pull towards isolation. It wasn't until my senior year in high school that this particular dream became a non-negotiable goal. I didn't have a personal relationship with God, I'd just ended a romantic relationship of almost a year, and my friendships seemed to be crumbling into a dark abyss of nothingness. The flaws of other people began to shine brighter than anything else and a bitterness began to grow inside of me, and would eventually consume the entirety of my being. I began to hate people. That hatred drove me to the point of graduating a semester early so that I would no longer "have to be around them", and could live peacefully in isolation from my peers.

The first week of the spring semester, I was on cloud nine as all my former classmates were going back to school while I was merely dropping my brothers off and then driving back home to do navigate throughout my day as I pleased. I instantly began to spout out the pros of not being around people; no one to compare myself to, no one to make me angry, no one's feelings to hurt, no problems to fix, no one to annoy me, no difficulties, no pain, no nothing. As all of those "pros" seemed to have some truth to them, the isolation didn't last for long. Little by little I got to the point to where I thought I was going to lose my mind if I didn't get out and be around people. The only flaw in that turn of events was that I only reached out to my friends was because I thought I was going to go mad if I didn't. I wasn't in a place, spiritually, where I could see what exactly God was trying to show me.

So fast-forward about 3 ½ years and I am going into my third year of college, still finding myself dreaming of moving away and getting an apartment in a city where I do not know anyone, or even have the desire to. Except for this time, it was simply a desire in my heart and I couldn't pinpoint why the thought of it seemed so pleasing to me. I loved all of my friends, peers, pastors, co-workers, and people I had surrounding me at the time, and did not want to live life without them. I began to think about how difficult and lonely life would be if I were to follow through with that desire. Instantly, God brought me to Genesis 2:18 "The Lord God said, "It is not good for man to be alone..." Then he began to reveal to me the importance of community. He reminded me that if humans allow themselves to be isolated, their own thoughts will very well eat them alive. We would:

1. Have trouble discerning God's voice.
2. Have trouble renouncing sin in our lives.
3. We would be giving the enemy a foothold in our lives.
4. We would become so independent that it would be hard to depend on God.
5. We would be conquered by loneliness.
6. We would have no accountability or someone to encourage growth.

And as if that weren't enough, the Lord then reminded me of my senior year in high school. He began to tell me the reason being surrounded by so many people brings so much insecurity, difficulties and pain are because satan knows it's not good for man to be alone. And because he knows that, he is going to do everything in his power to destroy community so that man would desire to be alone.

The enemy had been working to destroy community in my life since day one! He knew the power that would come from being surrounded by people (God's people especially), and he did not want that for me, or for any of God's children for that matter. But that is exactly why God was calling me to fight. God not only wants us to fight for the community, but he also wants us to fight against the schemes of the enemy. All of the negativity satan tries to plant through having friends and community can, and should be destroyed. Instead of comparing ourselves to others, why not lift others up and ask God to help us see ourselves the way He does?

Instead of avoiding relational conflict, why not hit it in the head, use patience, love, and wisdom to solve the problems in a healthy manner? Instead of getting irritated because someone annoyed us, why not be more concerned about what's going on in their life, that caused that person's behavior? God has an answer for every single excuse we try to give him about why we believe we are better off alone. He has the answer because He knows that we're not better off. He said it himself. How are you going to fight for the community today?

<u>Let's Pray</u>
God, thank you so much that I don't have to live life alone. Thank you for intentionally giving me people who you demonstrate your love for me. Thank you that I never have to be alone, because you will never leave me. Please help me to fight for the community in my life, as I realize it is a gift from you that is much needed. Please guide me in facing relational difficulties that the enemy tries to throw my way. I know that, with you, I can fight against every attack and win. I pray for wisdom and discernment so that I may treat people the way you would, and love the people I have a hard time loving. I do not want to do life alone and I am grateful I don't have to. When I have the desire to isolate myself, please give me strength and courage to reach out to someone I trust. You are almighty and all powerful, so I believe I can do all these things through your strength. Thank you for your grace, love, and mercy. Thank you for community! I love you and I love your people. Amen.

Secret Petition

"I waited and waited and waited for God, At last, He looked finally listened." - Psalm 40:1 (MSG)

Do you have a secret petition that only Jesus knows? Have you been waiting a long time for a prayer to be answered? Are you tired of praying?

Due to extenuating circumstances, after my mother's death, we went to live with one of our maternal aunts. Many years had passed and we lost contact with our Dad. He wanted to be part of our lives but our aunt didn't allow it. The times he did visit us; it was a barrage of insults against him. Her words were as a deadly weapon set to destroy him. The insults were brutal. He had no defense for Dad was guilty as charged, therefore he decided it was best not to visit us anymore. Years later, I found out this was the most heart-breaking decisions he made.

Secretly, I prayed every night that I would see my Dad. The days turned into weeks, the weeks turned into months, and the months turned into years. I didn't see any evidence that my secret petition would be answered but I never gave up hope. You see hope is not only an emotion but the hope is Christ himself.

One morning in the spring of my junior year in high school, the alarm clock didn't go off. This event precipitated everything to go "off" in my day. I woke up late and I missed my train, the trains were delayed. To say the least, I was not a happy camper. The next train pulled into station 25 minutes later. To my amazement when the train's door opened, there was my dad. My heart was full of joy. Dad didn't take the subway. He usually drove everywhere. This particular morning, he had an appointment at the VA hospital. His car broke down "mysteriously" and he had no choice but to take the train. An unscheduled father and daughter reunion orchestrated by the Lord.

Since then I have traveled much but that was the best train ride in my life. The Lord heard my cry. He made my secret petition come true. My faith in Christ skyrocketed, to say the least. This propelled me to continue to pray for all matters in my life whether big or small. A new level of intimacy developed between Jesus and me. Jesus can be trusted. Hence I learn not only to pray for my concerns but for others too. My friend, don't lose hope, keep praying, and keep believing! The Lord hears each petition. Your answer is on its way. The least unexpected moment you will receive your answer. You will feel surprised and joy at the same time.

Let's Pray
Abba God, you hear the secret petition in our hearts. You hear the very petition we cannot utter with words. Lord, you know the deep longings in our hearts. Oftentimes, waiting for an answer is long and lonely. Lord, you are the only one that can answer our prayers. As we wait for the answer grant us your strength. Grant us your grace to keep believing and praying. Your grace that enables us to keep asking until we see the answer. In Jesus' name Amen.

Trusting Others = Trusting God

Do you believe that God is working all things together for your good? Lately, I haven't had any trouble trusting that God holds true to that, or any of his promises. However, I have had every single problem trusting a man because I know we've all fallen short of the glory and will continue to do so. I know we, as a human race, mess up and do not love as well as God does. But this morning God told me if I fully trusted in him, I'd allow myself to trust in man. Why? Because even if (and when) man lets me down, my security would still be found in God and God alone. Any and all evil that forces itself in my direction, from being let down by man, will be restored by none other than Jesus Christ. Man will always fail me but Christ never will, and he's there comforting me when man is merely being what man is; imperfect.

This is not to say I should place all of my hope in man, and rely on man to meet the needs only God can, but say I don't have to be afraid of being let down. No matter how someone comes against me, I know that He will fight that battle because I am not meant to. I can trust that God is never surprised, and he is already working an attack into something completely beautiful; for my good.

So, I am going to trust today. I am going to trust in a restoration that will come after let-downs. I am going to trust in my God who can and will turn every mess into a beautiful work of art. And in doing those things I will experience events I would have never come across if I chose to not allow myself to be vulnerable. If you struggle with trusting those around you, I encourage you to look for your security in God alone.

Proverbs 3:5 "Trust in the Lord with all your heart; lean not on your own understanding and he will make your paths straight."

Let's Pray

God, I thank you for being sovereign. I can trust that you will never let me down, because you are absolutely perfect, and for that I am grateful. Help me to trust in you with all of my heart, not just the parts I choose to trust you with. I don't want to lean on my own understanding of people or the world anymore. My understanding doesn't compare to yours, so help me to seek after yours. I want to see people, situations and myself the way you see me. I know that you can take me further if I trust the people you have given me. I also know that if someone comes against me, you will work things out for my good. Thank you that I do not have to be afraid of let-downs, but please help me to use wisdom in my day-to-day conversations. I want to say only what you would want me to say, and do only what you would want me to do because only then will my path be set straight. I trust you, God. I trust you no matter what happens in my human interactions. You are high above it all, and you have the power to make any and all mess beautiful. I trust you with all of my heart. I trust you and I love you. Amen.

Please Don't Forget Me

Petitioning please don't forget me, was a prayer I often spoke right before I went to sleep before my head hit the pillow. It was acknowledging a person I knew of but did not follow. During those days I wasn't a confessing Christian, but those were the words which resided in my heart and out of a young lady in her twenties; who yearned to be acknowledged and loved. Thinking, "remember me? The one they kept looking over?" Because I refused to cry in front of those who often insulted me, it came across as "me having no feelings". I felt the world wanted to see me crack, just like my mother and those who oppressed me in school.

My mother, who emotionally and physically abused me, and later on accepted Christ, was part of me feeling neglected. Even the very place that seemed to be safe, the church, in which I often visited with my grandparents was tainted. There I found bullies as well as someone who violated my innocence; a person who was very well respected among the church leaders and admired by his family. I must say, it made me develop a tough shield which I often used to keep me going. My daughter, whom I had at 17, paid a severe price; I couldn't love her. I grew cold and neglectful of my emotional responsibilities. I lacked the tenderness and support of a mother. I thought this would be my mother's second chance to redeem herself to me, through my daughter, which was fine by me. I moved out of my mother's home leaving her the responsibility of raising my daughter for a short period of time. I continued to live a single life, after leaving my daughter's father who was verbally and physically abusive throughout our six-year relationship.

Even though I masqueraded myself as a strong, independent woman, inside of me remained a tender spot reserved for the one I longed to know. The night life I had wasn't enjoyable. How could one enjoy life without having the joy of being saved? Joy is an emotion given by the Holy Spirit, something I wanted to have, but didn't know how to obtain. I couldn't go to the church, I was scarred.

I refused to follow the lineage of witchcraft in my generation. I believed in the supernatural, but Santeria wasn't the way to know God. It was frightening to know that at any moment I could slip into eternal damnation.

I found myself not worth redemption, battling with thoughts of "what if I become a hypocrite" going in and out of the church. I didn't want to do this alone and asked God to find me a husband, so we both can serve Him. By saying this, I knew that God would give me the compatible partner I needed. In October 1994, I met my husband during a women's night out at a local club. It was a great feeling to meet someone that I was in sync with. A man who was a great listener, who focused on me, and shared the same religious beliefs. During a period of a year, I was engaged and then married. Shortly after our wedding day, I had an inclination to go to Puerto Rico; this being the same place I had my first encounter with Jesus. There were many prophetic dreams I had, which left a very grim feeling knowing I wasn't saved. During the plane ride, I remember speaking to the Lord saying "If you can't save me now, please just leave me alone". It was torturous to know the truth and feel it out of my reach. I needed help.

During my stay in Puerto Rico, I visited my godparents. Not knowing they were born again believers, we stood there a couple of days. They asked me to attend one of their gatherings to which I had said yes. As I listened attentively to the preacher, I began to cry. I wanted to say yes to salvation, but the fear of falling short of my commitment paralyzed me. At that moment, my husband, the alcoholic smoker, and the one I met in a club kneeled down and prayed. His prayer was simple; "Lord please save her". Seeing my husband speak to the Lord almost made me jealous. How could he be so confident to speak to Him? I felt like the thief on the cross, "Lord remember me when you enter your kingdom". That was the extent of my prayer. I felt like I wasn't worth His attention.

My husband approached the pastor, and at that moment he was asked the life-changing question. "Would you like to accept Jesus Christ as your Lord and Savior?" To where my husband boldly responded, "I accept Jesus Christ for me and my wife". I was bewildered and stunned. Through my husband's kindness, he had stripped me of my own personal invitation with Jesus. I witnessed my husband being touched by the Holy Spirit as I stood there in awe. I knew my husband couldn't accept Jesus Christ for me. I couldn't understand what happened. I was upset, feeling like my husband had beat me to it. The pastor then asked me if I wanted to be accepted, to which I said yes with uncertainty.

As I repeated the prayer of salvation, I heard an inner voice say "Kneel down before me Haydee". I refused to take heed of this voice, almost as if I was fighting myself. Again I heard "Kneel down before me Haydee" and resisted until I felt a power that forced me to my knees. It was my pride that fought the voice, I know that now. I was the one resisting His call. In all my rebellion and resistance of his call, He supplied me with a helper, my husband, and the power for me to say yes. He did remember me.

Let's Pray
I speak unto any uncertainties that you may have about your salvation. I come up against the whispers of the enemy, saying you will go back to the familiar; that you are too weak to continue the race. I speak unto you boldness and strength for any challenges that may come your way. You have what it takes. You are Gods elected and He does not forget his daughters. Amen

Freedom

"Freedom is never voluntarily given by the oppressor; it must be demanded by the oppressed."
–Dr. Martin Luther King, Jr.

Accepting Every Season in Life

At the time of writing this, the previous year was the biggest year of my life thus far. Six months ago I graduated college, started my first "big girl" job, and married the love of my life. Those are all great things, right? Most people would say that makes me accomplished for the age of 22. The reason I tell you all of that is because it was actually the 6 months following where I learned the most.

My entire life I've always been a goal oriented person. If I say I'm going to do something, I'm going to do it. For example, I decided at a young age that I was going to get a bachelor's degree and for the last 10 years or so that was what I worked toward. I worked very hard in high school to get accepted into college, and once I got there I worked even harder to stay and get my degree done in four years. I supported myself, at times working three jobs to support myself and maintain my school schedule. I was a commuter student in college and had to drive 100 miles a day to back and forth. There were semesters where I would get out of class at almost 10:00 PM, drove an hour to get home and had to wake up by 5:00 AM the next day to drive through rush hour traffic to be back to school for an 8:00 AM class. My last two semesters, I also planned a wedding while being a full-time student. So basically, I worked so hard to achieve my goals. Sure, I learned a lot in that time like, how to rely on God for strength and how to be humble during a huge year in my life. The year was hard at times but extremely exciting. It wasn't until after all of that was over that I learned the most.

After my honeymoon, I remember sitting on my couch feeling guilty because I did not have anything to do. Of course, I had to be a wife, but I didn't have a paper to write, a test to study for, or wedding projects to do. I automatically started thinking about what I was going to do next. The thing was, I didn't know what I was going to do. I didn't include this little detail before, but that "big girl" job I started; it wasn't a job using my four-year college degree that I worked so hard to get. I ended up taking a job at a place that my heart truly loved, and I really felt like God put that job in my path for a reason. I loved my job, but it was so hard to accept that I was doing a job that wasn't using my degree in Speech Pathology. I started thinking about what my next college degree would be. If God didn't want me to use that degree, then what degree was I supposed to have? I think we all have times in our lives where we question what God is doing, this season was definitely one of those times for me. People would constantly ask me "what's next?" and it killed me not to have a new goal to achieve. It wasn't until roughly four months later that I realized what God was really doing.

God was trying to teach me a lesson that I never had to learn before. God was trying to teach me to be patient and to accept where I was. God had taught me so much about hard work and perseverance, but I had never had to be complacent before in my life and that took a while to accept. I was very confused as to why God wouldn't want me to keep achieving goals; it was what I've always been good at. Once I got to a point where I could really acknowledge what God was doing in my life, I began to learn and become receptive of the little things revealed, like being patient, releasing ego and understanding that it was okay not to have a "next step" moment. I learned about being a wife and had to rely on God for guidance in those moments. I am sure if you're married you know how much you learn in the first year of being. I found myself leaning on God more than ever before, even though I wasn't nearly as stressed or busy as I was in the previous season of my life.

I share this in hopes of showing that sometimes God will take us through different seasons in our lives. Some seasons are less comfortable than others, but once we fully learn to acknowledge God in those times we can learn a lot. I hope that you can also learn to accept every season that God takes you through.

"Have I not commanded you? Be strong and courageous. Do not be afraid; do not be discouraged, for the LORD your God will be with you wherever you go." Joshua 1:9 (NIV)

Below is an idea for a prayer to use. Please feel free to use these words, or use them as an idea of what to say during your reflection time with God.

Let's Pray

God, first, I want to thank you for every season that you bring me through in life. I realize that this season may be a little harder for me to accept than others that you have brought me through. At this time, I ask for your strength and guidance. I ask that you would help me keep my eyes and heart open to all of the wonderful things that you are going to teach me during this time. I also want to thank you for never failing me, thank you for always being there when I am ready to listen and accept whatever it is you are trying to teach me. I pray all of this in your Jesus name.

Bound to be Set Free

Bound by the Insanity,
Bound by the Lies,
Bound by the Insecurities,
that live deep inside.
Bound by the Hate
and the Pain that lingers on,
Bound to a Life that has no Purpose to go on.
Now.
Set Free from the Insanity,
Set Free from the Lies,
Set Free from the Insecurities,
that Lived deep inside.
Set Free from the Hate
and the Pain that lingered on,
Set Free to Live a life with a Purpose and a Cause.

Have you ever felt trapped, maybe by past circumstances or by deep pains haunting you at every moment? Isn't it amazing how hurtful words can be? How powerful our tongues can strike to the core of a being? We all have heard the phrase, "Sticks and stones may break my bones, but words will never hurt me". However, we all know that phrase is far from the truth. Whether it was something said to us long ago in our childhood, something we heard every day, a word from a friend or significant other or even things said passive aggressively, our words have the power to build up or destroy. Growing up, I experienced berating of the tongue. Much of my childhood is a blur and most memories are filled with pain.

My father passed away when I was six and a year later my mother started dating my now step-dad, and three years later they married. Looking back now I understand why he acted the way he did. However, for a long time, I didn't understand. The love of a father was absent for me and instead of fatherly love I experienced much micromanaging, anger, jealousy and verbal abuse. I thought it was normal to be treated and talked to in such a demeaning manner; I didn't know any different.

I was very quiet and shy as a child and was a perfect student in school. I never got in trouble and managed to retain A's and B's throughout my schooling. When I became a teenager, I was part of a youth group and went to church regularly. It was as if I was living a double life because I never shared with anyone the things that were said to me or the things I experienced behind closed doors. I always put on a smile and never let on that anything was bothering me. It wasn't until the latter part of my teens I realized that what was going on in my home was abnormal. Especially compared to some of my close friend's home life. Unfortunately, by now much of the damage had been done.

When you are in an environment for so long, beaten down and told you are nothing, the inevitable happens; you start to believe it. As a result, insecurities were at all time high, relationships were a struggle, and at every moment I was thinking what's wrong with me? I hid all the pain, the baggage and the constant negative thoughts that reeled over and over in my head. On the outside, I continued to smile and put on a happy face. I faked being ok. I was afraid to let anyone in and found it very hard to believe that I was worthy of anyone's love, attention or affection. My very close friends would try to tell me differently, but it went in one ear and out the other. The worst part was hearing messages, sermons and even other fellow believers talk about how much Jesus loves us, that He wants a relationship with us and wants to restore us. I didn't believe them. After years and years of being belittled from a father figure, how was I supposed to believe that my so-called Heavenly Father, loved me?

After many years of pretending I was ok, I hit the bottom while in college and it seemed to come out of nowhere. I'd been in a relationship that had gone south and with the pressures of schoolwork along with the other emotional baggage I carried, I couldn't go on. My own strength was failing me and I didn't know what to do. My body then started physically ailing, I was depressed and beyond miserable, yet it was hard for me to pinpoint what was wrong. It's very hard to understand and explain this type of pain unless one has experienced it. I was a Christian at this point in my life; however, I had tried life on my own for so long and was so overwhelmed with my baggage that I couldn't clearly think to call on the Lord. Thankfully I had a roommate who could spiritually discern that something was wrong and told me about a church program called Celebrate Recovery. Honestly, I didn't want to go. I know that may sound crazy as if I had other options, but she took me kicking and screaming the entire way. I kept thinking in my mind what was Jesus going to do for me? He didn't love me, did He? Would He really help me? After finally realizing that I wasn't able to fix my problems, or myself, I relented and decided to go through with the program. It was an extremely slow and painful process, but in the end, it was worth it. I learned how to build a relationship with the Lord, I learned that I could be restored and learned how to stop listening and believing the lies of the enemy. Most importantly I learned that Jesus did love me, He wasn't angry and wanted a relationship with me. I didn't have to be a victim of my circumstances anymore and I came to understand my true value, through having a deep relationship with the Lord and reading his Word.

Dear sister, does any of this apply to you? If so, know that you don't have to be a victim of your circumstances. Your worth is not based on what people may have called you. The enemy wants you to believe all the lies that have been spoken about you or to you. John 10:10 ESV says, "The thief comes only to steal and kill and destroy". The enemy wants to destroy you and your potential. He wants you to believe you are nothing, that you are useless. If he has you believing the lies, then he has you ineffective for the Kingdoms work. But there is hope! If you continue reading John 10:10 Jesus says, "I came that they may have life, and have it abundantly." The Lord has much planned for you and wants a relationship with you and if the enemy can get you to believe otherwise, he will. Take a moment and reflect on your own life. Is there any pain or baggage that you have been carrying? If that is the case, I want to encourage you to take all your pain, baggage and lies you've believed, to the foot of the cross. Maybe you're thinking, how do I do that or what does that even look like? Confession! Confess anything and everything that was said to you and about you. Tell someone, write it down and get it out. Don't hold on to the pain any longer. The enemy wants to keep you in bondage, but when you confess, chains start to break. It's ok if you don't "feel" anything. It's not about feelings, it's about confessing. Find a church if you don't have one and get connected. Find someone you know and trust that is a strong believer and talk to them. Look for any recovery or support groups at church to plug into as well. Completely submerging yourself with Jesus and fellow believers is the beginning of the journey. It will take time, lots of time, but it will be worth it. Whenever you doubt His love or redemption go to the Word.

Here are some scriptures to meditate on when in doubt and need some encouragement.

"Come to Me, all who are weary and heavy-laden, and I will give you rest." Matthew 11:28 (ESV)

"My soul, wait in silence for God only, For my hope is from Him. He only is my rock and my salvation, My stronghold; I shall not be shaken." Psalm 62:5-6 (NASB)

"Therefore if anyone is in Christ, he is a new creature; the old things passed away; behold, new things have come." 2 Corinthians 5:17 (ESV)

"Are not two sparrows sold for a cent? And yet not one of them will fall to the ground apart from your Father. But the very hairs of your head are all numbered. *So do not fear; you are more valuable than many sparrows." Matthew 10:29-31 (NASB)*

"For You formed my inward parts; You wove me in my mother's womb. I will give thanks to You, for I am fearfully and wonderfully made..." Psalm 139:13-14 (NASB)

Let's Pray
Heavenly Father I lift my sister up to you now. Father, you see her hurt, you see her pain and the lies she has come to believe. I ask Lord that she finds her worth in You! I ask that she realizes through your word and through your Holy Spirit how much she is loved and how worthy she is because you call her daughter. Lord reveal the deep seeded roots and lies from the enemy. Devil, you are a liar and in the name of Jesus, every chain, every stronghold and every root must be broken. I ask that you would preserve her Lord and restore her to you. I Thank You for loving, even when we don't feel it or realize it. I ask Lord that You would comfort my sister during this time and wrap your arms of love and peace around her. I thank you for hearing our prayers and I ask all these things in Jesus name, Amen!

The King Who Saved Me

Have you ever felt like something was missing, like, there was more to life? Have you ever thought what's wrong with me? Or how could I make my life better?

There was a point in my life where I was easily distracted by the things of the world and was lost. When things in my life went wrong, every part of me felt empty, chaotic and hopeless. I didn't know how to cope with life in a positive way and would get mad at those around me, talk ugly about them or want to fight with them. I knew who God was an associate of mine. I affiliated Him with my needs only and didn't know him as a friend. I didn't see Him as someone to walk and talk with daily and only called on him when I needed something. I did many of the things that unbelievers do.

I broke most of the 10 commandments (Exodus 20:1-17) that God spoke of. He commanded us not to have other Gods, but I did. I worshiped my clothes, my money, my jewelry, and other worldly items more than God. I used His name in vain countless times and didn't honor my mother and father. I murdered people with my words and my actions. I lied, cheated, and stole. I still can remember the day I almost got arrested for stealing clothing from a popular department store like it was yesterday, but by God's grace, I didn't go to jail. Even when I didn't understand who He was, He was watching over me.

I didn't think twice about what God expected of me or the life He had planned for me. I went to church off and on and listened to the preacher, but I didn't take what was said to heart. I didn't live it out, and honestly, I don't think I knew how. There came a point in my life when I was looking for more than the world had to offer. One Sunday morning while I was at church, my heart was heavy with grief from life's disasters and pain. As the preacher continued, I felt this overwhelming surge of tears that began to well up in my eyes. While the tears rolled down my face, the preacher began to make an altar call asking if anyone wanted to give their heart to

Rise Up to Greatness

Jesus. At that moment I wanted my heart to have peace and my tears lead me down the aisle of the church, where I gave my life over to Jesus. I accepted him into my heart and He became my good friend. But I didn't quite understand what God's plan was for me at the time.

A couple of years went by and I slowly stop going to church due to various things going on in my life. I started out strong, but that quickly faded as situations arose day by day. I felt like Peter in Matthew 14:29 when he walked on water and lost focus because he took his eyes off Jesus. He began to sink! I had taken my eyes off Jesus too and I was slowly sinking. I began straddling the fence of wanting what the world offered and what Jesus offered. The world still had a hold on me.

About a year later, a friend of my husband invited our family to church. We enjoyed the experience and continued to go there. My heart's desire began to change. The more I went and fellowshipped with the other believers, the more I began to realize the plan God wanted for me (Jeremiah 29:11). I saw the difference of the people in that church who were around me. They knew Jesus and took His word very seriously. They had built their life on a rock solid foundation with God at the center. When life situations came, they were unmovable! They continued on a road of peace.

I'd made my mind up that I wanted that same rock solid foundation made through and by God. My eyes, my ears, and my heart were open for everything and anything that God was offering me. I began to change the way I thought about life. I approached each situation and circumstance with God in mind. I began to study His word. Instead of getting mad and sulking in my feeling, I began to take my troubles and cares to God in prayer. In return, He gave me peace and showed me a way out of disastrous situations.

I started to understand that I'd been the foolish one who God spoke of in Matthew 7:27. Each time I went to church and heard the word, I was building my life on a foundation of sand. We all know that sand isn't stable and can be blown by the wind or carried downstream by the flow of the water in an instant. I never put the words of God into practice. And my life was like sand and the situations we're the water or the wind that caused chaos. Since I have put God in the center of my life and everything I do is with Him in mind, I am strong and secure in life's day to day occurrences. No more of being wiped out by life situations! Jesus was missing and the one I needed more of. He is the one who made my life better.

A few scriptures to meditate on:
"For I know the plans I have for you," declares the LORD, "plans to prosper you and not to harm you, plans to give you hope and a future." Jeremiah 29:11 (NIV)

Come," he said. Then Peter got down out of the boat, walked on the water and came toward Jesus. But when he saw the wind, he was afraid and, beginning to sink, cried out, "Lord, save me!" Matthew 14:29-30(NIV)

"Therefore everyone who hears these words of mine and puts them into practice is like a wise man who built his house on the rock. The rain came down, the streams rose, and the winds blew and beat against that house, yet it did not fall, because it had its foundation on the rock. But everyone who hears these words of mine and does not put them into practice is like a foolish man who built his house on sand. The rain came down, the streams rose, and the winds blew and beat against that house, and it fell with a great crash." Matthew 7:24-27(NIV)

"Trust in the Lord with all your heart and lean not on your own understanding; in all your ways submit to him, and he will make your paths straight." Proverbs 3:5-6(NIV)

Let's Pray
Lord, I thank you for the reader of the above words. I know that it is not by chance that they read this message, but that you had a divine appointment for them. Just like you had a plan for my life, you have a plan with purpose for them too. I ask that you would work in their heart, so that they may draw closer to you and walk hand and hand as I do and even closer. Allow them to be loose from the strongholds that misalign them with you. I pray that they would trust in you

Lord with all their heart, and lean not on their own understanding, but submit to you so that their paths can be made straight as it is written in Proverbs 3:5-6. In Jesus mighty name, I pray, Amen!

Steps to Freedom

Where the spirit of the Lord is there is freedom, right? Yes! But often times we prevent ourselves from receiving that freedom. Personally, the specific bondage that was holding me back from receiving the freedom God was unforgiveness. I'd had been harboring unforgiveness toward my biological father for as long as I could remember. He was in and out of my life, claimed I wasn't his child and showed an extreme amount of inconsistency in my life.

Upon going to Southwestern Assemblies of God University, in Waxahachie, Texas, I thought I forgave him after the Lord revealed to me the bitterness I had toward him. However, while sitting in the sanctuary at a "Freedom Weekend" The Oaks Fellowship holds, the Lord tugged on my heart, shining light on the unforgiveness I had tucked away, and failed to give completely to Him. The very first thing I acknowledged was the Lord's presence there in that room. I gave thanks to Him for all He is and then committed myself to His will and not my own. It was then He began to wreck me and showed me I accepted the lie that love wasn't real because I didn't receive it from my earthly father. I'd also accepted the lie that every man that came into my life would leave me. These were lies that had affected every single decision I had made up until that point. But God is so good that He not only told me these things, but He revealed to me the root of the hurt. I closed my eyes and God took me back to the very moment the seed of hatred and hurt towards my dad was planted.

There was a time in my life when my dad had made an effort to repair our relationship. I still had walls up, but he was making progress in breaking them down. On this specific day, he had promised to take me to school on Halloween, so I sat in the living room anxiously awaiting his arrival. As the time he promised to be there passed, my heart began to sink lower and lower into my stomach. My mom, disappointed, then suggested I start heading to the bus stop because I still had time to catch it. As I tried my hardest to hold in the hurt, I began to walk down the long stretch towards the bus stop. But just as quick as I was walking, I came to a complete halt the instance that I saw the bus drive right past my stop. The tears began to drown out every part of me—I didn't have enough time to make it. It was in that moment something inside of me broke and didn't receive healing until the moment of my spiritual encounter.

It amazed me how satan used such a simple experience to distort my view of love, and even fill my heart with hatred toward my father. But through this, God first taught me that forgiveness isn't for the other person, but freedom for myself. It doesn't mean their actions were okay and it isn't forgetting what they did. It is, however, a choice.

A choice to acknowledge the hurt and hate, but no longer allowing those things to have power over you. It also is a choice to love that person regardless, since that is what we're called to do. With that being said, to love someone doesn't mean you allow them to have influence in your life. It could be as simple as lifting them up in prayer. God still wasn't done yet. He showed me His love was pure, real, and He showed me the root of my hurt leading me to forgive. God had one more thing to do, and that was to kill my pride. At first, I didn't want to give up being "strong" in not allowing my dad to feel forgiven.

As you can see, that affected me for years upon years. Even after I had told my father I had forgiven him, I still allowed the pride of "making it this far" without him to have a great hold on my life. To break free from that mentality I had to acknowledge that it was not God's will for me to withhold love from my dad, due to my own selfishness.

I declared to the Lord that I wanted His will for my life and not my own, and my guidance of my own life did not amount to his, and never would. After that declaration, I went home and reached out to my dad. I fully allowed him the permission to begin to build a fulfilling relationship with me. To this day, our relationship isn't what most would call a 'normal' father-daughter relationship, but it is a relationship where God's unconditional love reigns. It's restored and one that God is using for our good.

Galatians 5:1 "It is for freedom that Christ has set us free. Stand firm, then, and do not let yourselves be burdened again by a yoke of slavery."

Let's Pray
Jesus, thank you! Your love is pure. Your love is true. And most of all, your love is unconditional. I am so sorry I believed the lie that your love was not real, for so long. I did not accept the love you gave freely, and now I realize just how much I was missing out on. Thank you for shining light on the darkest parts of my heart. You've revealed things to me that I didn't even know were there, and that in itself shows just how much you really do love me. I thank you for the freedom I have in you, and the freedom I have in forgiving others. Thank you for blessing me with my earthly father, and allowing our relationship to be restored. Thank you for being a perfect father to me. I pray against any and all attacks from the enemy, not only in my own life but in my dad's life as well. I pray that your grace, forgiveness, comfort, and peace would flood into his life. Help me to better understand him, and to better love him. I give you any and all unforgiveness, pride or bitterness that may still be dwelling in my heart. Please lead me to other people dealing with this same struggle so that I may minister to them, as you have to me. Heal hearts and touch minds, Lord. Thank you for all that you do, and all that you are continuing to do. I love you. Amen.

Trim Your Hedges

"Every branch in Me that does not bear fruit He takes away; and every branch that bears fruit He prunes, that it may bear more fruit." John 15:2 (NKJV)

When I was younger and lived across the street from where my current home is, I resided next to neighbors that had a backyard full of trees. One day I actually counted (because when you are that age you have the time in your schedule to do things like count trees), and if I'm not mistaken, there were about 13 trees in one backyard. I never saw it as a problem, but the surrounding neighbors, including my parents, always expressed concern with the ridiculous amount of trees in one small backyard. I wondered why this was. Well, when a bad storm would hit, it wasn't out of the ordinary for branches and limbs from one of these trees to fall. So basically neighbors were concerned for the safety of themselves and their property. Me being the inquisitive child that I was then wondered why the trees were so fragile and breaking up everywhere. Come to find out, these trees were not properly cared for and were never pruned.

Pruning is defined as cutting or clearing things that are undesired. With trees, pruning is done so that the dead branches, roots, etc. (or undesirable material) can be removed to cause better growth and maintain the health of the tree. In other words, you have to get rid of the old, dead stuff to get new, fuller foliage, and prettier trees. So, like trees, we sometimes need to get rid of the old, dead stuff to become new in and grow in Christ. And growth has everything to do with being a Believer.

How can we grow if we do not trim the undesirable things from our lives and hold onto to them to the point where they choke out our purpose? One of the things that we as Believers often hold on to is our past. Sometimes we keep such a tight hold on our past that we allow it to stop us from progressing. Sometimes as Believers, we forget that the Bible says "old things are passed away" and that "all things have become new". We prevent God from pruning the old, dead stuff and allowing it to "pass away" when we hold on to it. Now don't get me wrong, by no means am I saying that we should forget our past. There are many things that we experience in our lives that are intended to make us stronger or teach us lessons that we are meant to carry for an extended amount of time. However, there is a difference between holding on to the lessons we have learned from our past and holding on to the parts of our past that make us feel unworthy of moving forward and fulfilling our God-given purpose.

In my senior year of college, I started struggling with depression. In addition to the academic expectations of senior year, I had also committed to a number of extracurricular tasks that I felt I was falling short with and becoming a disappointment. No matter what I tried, I was still unable to catch up in each area of my life and with each failed attempt, I grew wearier. Life had become so overwhelming that I felt hopeless and helpless. I began to seek counseling services to help me make sense of everything and in hopes of getting ahead of everything that had me feeling defeated. Oh, did I mention that I was studying psychology with the goal of being a psychologist? As I moved along in my studies and in managing my depressive symptoms, I questioned if I was equipped to help other people when I clearly didn't have it together emotionally myself. I continued my studies in psychology but started to think that it lacked purpose due to my internal struggles. After some time, I eventually came to the realization that my experiences didn't have to prevent me from helping others. I didn't have to hold onto it as though it was a scarlet letter of sorts. I realized that my past gave me a unique experience that would help me to be more empathic to my future clients. So, in this instance, I had to let go of the part of my past that was holding me back, and honor the part that was helping me be a blessing to others. Today, I can proudly say that I overcame that season in my life and use what I went through to empathize with my clients and empower them with the tools that need to overcome as well.

Let's Pray
Father God, thank you for your divine ability to make all things new. Thank you for using the things that once had us bound and turning them into the very things that propel us closer to our purpose. It's all so that you can get the glory, and we thank you for using our lives and our stories to encourage others and to draw people closer to you. God, please remind us that we overcome by the word of our testimonies, so when you give us the opportunity to share the things that you have delivered us from, give us the holy boldness needed to stir the spirits of others. Thank you for making us small pieces in the puzzle of life and allowing us to affect change in the lives of the others around us. In Jesus' name, Amen.

Mind Renewing Faith Lavished With Love

The road of life is constantly winding to and fro with many unexpected happenings that consist of hills of happiness and valleys of despair, but God is ever so good along the way. He is more than amazing. The reality is we have to be willing to put our trust completely in Him so He can lead the way on the road of life.

In my early 30s, all seemed well and life was good. Nothing could go wrong (at least I thought). I had everything I believed was beneficial and needed. I was living a pretty good life, nice home, good job, great church family, my family and I were healthy, and I had friends to mingle with. Life seemed at its best.

In the spring of 2012, I had decided to step out on faith and quit my job. I had a desire in my heart to spend more time with my kids. The life of a working mother was weighing me down emotionally and at times physically. I also made up my mind to homeschool my children because I wanted to educate my kids not only academically, but spiritually. A couple of months went by and all was well.

As the summer break was ending, my family and I ventured to Mexico on a vacation. We returned around mid-August with plans of beginning a new chapter in our life. I would be a stay at home mom who homeschooled. Plus, the excitement of coming back home to family and friends after being gone for over 2 weeks was overwhelmingly thrilling. We couldn't wait to share the awesome stories and pictures of our trip. And to add to the excitement, my 2nd oldest son was also celebrating a birthday. As we settled in the night before, my husband and I decided it would be a good idea to take the birthday boy to lunch. We let him choose the eating place and agreed afterward that he would pick two friends to venture to a local amusement/ game room venue. My husband decided he would skip the game venue so that he could catch up on work related stuff. In the process of being out for lunch with the birthday boy, a close girlfriend of mine at the time had called and agreed to keep me company while I chaperoned my son and his friends at the local game venue. My girlfriend and I laughed and talked as my son and his friends played games and enjoyed themselves. As the evening progressed, we stopped for a bite to eat and continued our conversation filled with laughter. My son and his friends were enjoying every bit of the evening of fun and game too. Just as we were preparing to leave the eatery, my girlfriend got really serious and declared that she had to tell me something. She started off asking did I think that my husband was faithful. Without a second thought, I answered "Yes". She went on to say how she thought he wanted her and that he had given her his phone number. At this point, the conversation seemed surreal. I remember going home that night feeling confused and shocked. I told my husband what happened and he couldn't believe the accusations this woman had made against him.

I never would've thought my life could shift in an instant from a few words spoken. I began questioning everything, in my mind, concerning my husband. Even though in my heart I felt that what this woman had said was untrue. My husband had never displayed or acted in any way of unfaithfulness. But somehow I let the enemy take over and capture my mind into believing otherwise.

    The school year was set to start within a week and my plans of homeschooling my children were never fulfilled. I thought at the time, it would be best for the kids to return to school because I was a mess. I began to battle with ideas of unfaithfulness in my mind to a point where I was unable to focus at times. I began to have anxiety attacks and spells of crying and felt that each day was a struggle. Life wasn't going as I had planned a few months earlier. I didn't want to be around others and I would constantly push my husband away. I was desperate for relief from the thoughts of my mind. At one point, I felt as though I needed to see a psychologist; this went on for months.

    I knew who God was and I knew that prayer worked. So daily I would drop my kids off at school and go home to spend time with God. I would lay on the floor in my room beside my bed praying and reading my Bible. Sometimes, all I could do was cry and just rest in His presence. I felt as if I needed to just lay in His arms and let God hold me. I needed to be reminded that He saved me once before from my sins and he would save me again this time from my roaming mind and thoughts that I was bombarded with from the enemy.

As months went by, I continued to pray that God would heal my mind, strengthen me, and He did. As I prayed daily, I came across 3 scriptures I quoted in my prayers and used them as my sword to help me claim victory in restoring peace in my mind.

"Love is patient and kind. Love is not jealous or boastful or proud or rude. It does not demand its own way. It is not irritable, and it keeps no record of being wronged. It does not rejoice about injustice but rejoices whenever the truth wins out. Love never gives up, never loses faith, is always hopeful, and endures through every circumstance." 1 Corinthians 13:4-8 (NLT)

"Consider it pure joy, my brothers, and sisters, whenever you face trials of many kinds because you know that the testing of your faith produces perseverance. Let perseverance finish its work so that you may be mature and complete, not lacking anything." James 1:2-4 (NIV)

"Put on the whole armor of God that ye may be able to stand against the wiles of the devil. For we wrestle not against flesh and blood, but against principalities, against powers, against the rulers of the darkness of this world, against spiritual wickedness in high places." Ephesians 6:11-12 (KJV)

It's funny how life plays out. I had put my trust in a person whose friendship I valued, only to be lead into a battle of the mind by her words. The Lord was patient in dealing with me as He lavished me with endless love, mercy, and grace. He knew exactly what I needed. He put me in the ideal situation, at the right time (at home, not working and alone all day to rest in his presence). God is so good. I just keep saying Hallelujah and give Him the highest praise of all. All I had to do was be willing to let him heal my heart and renew my mind. I thank Him because He is not a bias God and He will do the same for you no matter what you are going through.

Let's Pray

Lord, allow the reader of this message to draw closer to you, so that they may be able to stand against the traps of the enemy. You know every detail of their life, including the trials they face. Allow them to be aware of the demonic spirits that try to impose situations in their life that would possibly take them out. I pray that they would be encouraged take your word and use it to guard their hearts and minds. In Jesus name, Amen!

Epilogue

As I began to look up the definition of "Greatness" a lot of words came up. Words like first- rate, notable, exceptionally outstanding and highly significant. All of those words are wonderful but the definition that stood out the most for me was "always striving to be better, no matter what level of excellence you obtain. It is not just about being the best, it also about bringing out the best in those around you. I.e. taking the time to give back and serve your community and impact the world."

When the issues of life rear its head, it's hard to think about giving back or serving anyone. You just want the pain or whatever you're going through to stop. However, I have learned that "greatness" within can rise in the most uncomfortable situations. And, we all have the ability to "rise to greatness" more than once in our lifetime.

I remember my 1st rise at the age of 22. I had a baby boy, wasn't married, the father of my child decided he didn't want to be one and my mother suddenly passed away. I had to grieve her passing, be a mother, and figure out how I was going to give my baby the best life possible. My mother had always drilled into me the importance of going to college. I always dismissed it because I didn't think I was good enough to go. I struggled most of my school life and people at school said I wasn't at a particular level to succeed. Because they said it, they must be right, correct? However, when my mother passed away and my son's father disappeared, something rose up in me and said to try as well as fight.

I applied to college and I remember the admissions interview like it was yesterday. During that time, you had to take a writing test to see if you would be able to keep up with the level of academics ahead. Truthfully, I didn't do well on the test. Actually, I was never was a great writer, at least that's what I was told, so it wasn't a surprise when shared that I didn't score well. The admissions counselor asked me why I wanted to go to college. I told him that I wanted a better life for my son and that my mother passed with the dream of me attending one day. I believed I had try and also honor her memory of attending. The admissions counselor told me that my story was touching but I probably wouldn't graduate because I had poor writing skills. His response to me was like a gut punch in the stomach and I became very angry.

Now for the 'rise' part! I continued to enroll in school and attended. It was a rough start and I received a lot of F's at first. Those F's turned into D's! Those D's turned into C's! Those C's turned into B's! And, I got a few A's! I graduated with my Bachelors Degree in Human Services. Proceeded a few years later to earn my Master's Degree in the same major and now I am an author of 6 books and have helped countless people fulfill their dream of becoming an author. Let me not forget, in the interim of this happening, I found my Lord and Savior Jesus Christ! Talk about Rising Up!!

You've just read a little of my life's story and over 30 devotionals on how you can "Rise to Greatness" with Love, Pain, Spirit, Family, and Freedom. These authors have shared their hearts, minds, and spirits with you. I stand with them in saying, you can do it! Despite what may be going on in your life right now, please know that God is with you always. As you continue to rise, rest in Him, know that He loves you and His word rings true, "But those who wait upon GOD get fresh strength. They spread their wings and soar like eagles, they run and don't get tired, they walk and don't lag behind." (MSG)

Because you have read this book and you have the support of these authors, your next level of "greatness" is right around the corner. So what's next? Begin to read the reflective journal and dig deep within yourself and God's scriptures to find your way to own way to 'rise'. You got this! You can do it! Most importantly, The Lord has your back.

Blessings,
Robin Devonish

Co-Author Devotions

Shelly Cassady
Bound to be Set Free
Fearful
Letting Go
Suffering

Dr. Té Colston
Beware of the Weeds
Rotten Fruit
Salty
Trim Your Hedges

Earline Connolly
Enough is Enough!
Fight or Die!
One Nation Under God
Snake Bit

Rikeisha Cunningham
Conquering Loneliness
The 6th Love Language
The Fight for Community
Trusting Others = Trusting God

Maria DiCroce
Reclaimed My Marriage

Ericka Felker
His Joy!
It is Possible

Rise Up to Greatness

Haley Graham
Accepting Every Season in Life
Jesus is Enough!

Ruth Hernandez
Laughter
Losing Someone Special
Secret Petition

Haydee Muniz
Just in Time
Remember Me

Sherree Olalde
Mind Renewing Faith with Lavished Love
The King Who Saved Me!

Selina Sosa
He Wants Your Worship
It's Going to be Okay!
My Years of Fears
The Invisible Image of God
Unconditional Love

About the Authors

Selina Sosa

Selina Sosa wants to live in a world where young Latina women are not boxed into the idea that there is only one way to succeed and that regardless of their ethnicity they can accomplish all of their goals.

As Founder of Ethnic Perspective, she is passionately encouraging young women to define their own ideas of success by means of entrepreneurship through, encouragement, and education and mentoring. When she's not spending time assisting others on their personal goals, Selina enjoys spending time with her family, going on vacations and staying physically fit.

Her next few endeavors are becoming a certified personal trainer, obtaining her credentialed for ministry and chaplaincy while also pursuing a degree in Cultural Studies.

Selina Sosa has been married for 22 years Fernando Sosa, and has three sons Justin, Elijah & Jeremiah Sosa.

Shelly Cassady

Shelly Cassady is currently an educator in the Texas public school system and resides in Dallas, Texas. She is also the Vice President of Ethnic Perspective.
In her free time she enjoys exercising and spending time with family and friends. Shelly also enjoys helping others and making a difference in the lives of those around her.

She holds a Bachelor in Exercise Science from the University of Texas at Austin and a Masters in Education from Texas A&M Commerce.
Her favorite Bible verse is Psalm 73:26, "My flesh and my heart may fail, but God is the strength of my heart and my portion forever."

Dr. Té Colston

Dr. Té Colston is a Doctor of Psychology with over 10 years of clinical experience and a licensed minister with experience serving youth, young adults, women and the incarcerated. She is passionate about spreading awareness about mental health and shedding a "psychological light" on a variety of topics, such as trauma, help-seeking behaviors and religious coping.

She is a Counselor for the City University of New York and Adjunct Assistant Professor at LIU Post.

Whether she is in a professional or ministerial setting, her goal is always to be a resource to others and to help them achieve the best state of mental health possible.

Earline Connolly

Earline is in covenant with her husband Kevin and co-steward of their daughter Maegan. She currently serves as a Board Member of Open Arms of Central Texas and is a co-founder and Marketing/Development Director for Restoring the Captives Ministry. Earline is an ordained minister of the Gospel specializing in women's ministries and equipping the lay community to be effective in their efforts to minister life and hope to those behind bars.

She has also developed a curriculum "Beauty for Ashes, the Metamorphosis of a Godly Woman", which is geared toward helping women reach their potential in ministry, marketplace, marriage, and life. She co-founded PWC, "Prison Wives Club", a support group for wives of family members who are incarcerated and in need of support for themselves

while their loved ones serve prison terms. Earline has designed a creative arts program for women who want to share their artistic gifts and talents with women who are incarcerated.

Earline and her husband Kevin minister to couples

who desire to build strong marriages during the separation of their incarceration. Earline is committed to expanding the Kingdom of God to the unlovable and untouchables of society.

Rise Up to Greatness

Rikeisha Cunningham

Rikeisha Cunningham is a sister of 5 brothers and a daughter to a hard-working mother. She left her home state, Colorado, to follow the Lord's call and attend college in Dallas, Texas. She is now a Junior at Southwestern Assemblies of God University, working on her Master's Degree in Organizational Leadership, and Bachelor's Degree in Church Leadership. She interns at The Oaks Fellowship, in a Student Development track, is on the board of directors for Ethnic Perspective and is a personal trainer at the YMCA.

Her hobbies include working out, writing, hiking, playing sports and learning about nutrition. She plans to create a pathway for Juvenile Delinquents to change the way they are seen, and work their way to a more successful future.

Maria DiCroce

Maria DiCroce has made a career in the fitness industry tying her faith into her guidance and council to help others be the best they can be inside and out.

A wife of 32 years to her loving husband Paul, a mother to 3 daughters and a grandmother (aka Gaga) to 4 granddaughters, Maria finds that even married after 32 years you will always need a tune up here and there if you want your marriage to last and shine the light.

Being part of this devotional has helped her to share her story so that others may be blessed.

Ericka Felker

Ericka Felker was born in Fort Dix, New Jersey but got to Texas at 6 weeks old and has been a resident ever since! She was adopted at the age of two along with her twin brother and raised by an amazing, strong woman of God and a father who was a DJ at a radio station in Dallas Texas.

Writing since she was a child, Ericka believes that she is now in a season of life where God is showing and preparing her for another level. Ericka says, "As I journey through the calling of God, He has placed much on my heart through writing. I pray my words, touch, and change, bring answers, bring freedom, encourages, inspires and brings the reader to a new image of God."

Wife, mother of 4 and Grammy to 1 is what cherishes the most. And, she enjoys the outdoors, adventure, road trips and coffee. Her motto is, "Always choose joy and remember you have victory in God! He is always with us and loves us so much!"

Haley Graham

Haley Graham is 23 years old, a wife, and currently an Administrative Assistant. She is from Waxahachie Texas, and holds a bachelors degree from the University of Texas at Dallas.

She currently serves as a small Group Leader at her church, working with 11th graders. She is very passionate about health and fitness, and is currently working on getting a certification to become a Personal Trainer. She loves dogs, and enjoys spending time with the two that she has at home. She aspires to show Jesus to others through her actions every day.

Her favorite Bible verse is Hebrews 12:11 "No discipline seems pleasant at the time, but painful. Later on, however, it produces a harvest of righteousness and peace for those who have been trained by it."

Ruth Hernandez

Ruth Hernandez gave her life to the Lord Jesus Christ at the age of ten years old after the loss of her mother and has never looked back. She has served the body of Christ as a deacon and leader for over 30 years. In 2007 she became a chaplain and has made herself available to every opportunity to minister the Gospel of Jesus Christ to the sick, the prisoner and anyone who would listen.

Ruth is a member of Elohim Christian Church in Queens New York and the leader of the prison ministry alongside her wonderful husband Hector Hernandez. Ruth's greatest accomplishment in this life in her opinion is being a wife to Hector Hernandez for nearly 25 years.

Ruth holds a bachelor's degree in Human Services and has worked at Mount Sanai Hospital for over 16 years in the Administrative field. She also has a degree Christian Education from the Spanish Eastern District (SED) Bible Institute.

Haydee Muniz Rivera

Rev. Haydee Rivera and her husband Jesus M. Rivera have been married for 22 years and have 3 vibrant daughters. For the past 5 years, they've been pastors at By His Grace Fellowship Church in Brooklyn, New York.

Haydee is an animal lover, with a special affinity toward cats. She reaffirms and encourages those that have been scattered and passionately abides by their church statement, "Connecting through our weaknesses, so that together in Him, we are made strong."

Sherree Olalde

Sherree Olalde is an early childhood teacher who enjoys helping young minds grow and blooms into successful learners.

Sherree leads a weekly prayer group called "Prayerful Friday". She is a wife and a mother of 4, who loves and serves the Lord.

www.ingramcontent.com/pod-product-compliance
Lightning Source LLC
Chambersburg PA
CBHW072050290426
44110CB00014B/1622